**Industrial
Location
in the
United States**

Charles River Associates Incorporated
is a professional service organization
in Cambridge, Massachusetts, that
specializes in economic and econometric research. CRA has conducted
research in the fields of transportation,
pollution control and abatement, and
natural resource industries, among
others. CRA's work is generally performed for long-range planning and
policy formulating groups in industry
and government.

Industrial Location in the United States

A Charles River Associates Research Study

An Econometric Analysis

James C. Burrows
Charles E. Metcalf
John B. Kaler

Charles River Associates
Incorporated

Heath Lexington Books
D.C. Heath and Company
Lexington, Massachusetts

Table of Contents

List of Tables

Preface

This monograph is based on a study performed by the authors at Charles River Associates. The original study was entitled *Area Employment Prediction to Determine Public Facilities Requirements,* prepared for the Economic Development Administration, U.S. Department of Commerce, Washington, D.C., under Contract C-315-65, January 1968.

The contents of this book reflect solely our views and we are entirely responsible for the accuracy of the data, conclusions, and analysis presented. The views expressed here do not necessarily reflect the views of the federal government, any agency thereof, or the publisher.

We wish to express our thanks to those persons who contributed to the initial report and to the final manuscript of the book. We are indebted to the Office of Economic Research of the Economic Development Administration, particularly to Robert Miki, EDA's technical representative on the project. We would also like to thank Philip Saunders, who made important contributions to the early research, particularly in the areas of the special models for agriculture and mining and of linking county forecasts to rational economic forecasts, and Richard Cherry, who directed all the computer programming and data processing. We are especially indebted to Gerald Kraft, president of Charles River Associates, and to Franklin M. Fisher of the Massachusetts Institute of Technology, who were instrumental in the development and statistical estimation of the model. Other members of CRA, especially Alan R. Willens, played important roles in the preparation of the original study. Finally, we would like to thank John R. Meyer of Yale University, who contributed a number of useful suggestions in the preparation of the final manuscript.

It is difficult to assign credit to any individual in a project as complex and as long in duration as the one described in this book. John Kaler, now with the Office of Economic Research of EDA, originally conceived the project and coordinated much of the research. James Burrows and Charles Metcalf participated jointly in the specification and estimation of the forecasting model and in the preparation of the report. The discussion of the cross-section problem and the problems unique to discriminant function can be attributed primarily to Charles Metcalf and the literature review and development of special industry models can be attributed primarily to James Burrows.

We feel that this monograph provides a significant contribution to the field of regional economics. We have attempted to point out the errors that can be made in analyzing industrial growth at the regional or subregional level and have developed a forecasting model that is free of most of these errors. We hope that this study will play a useful role in the development of the methodology of regional research.

James C. Burrows
Charles E. Metcalf
John B. Kaler

**Industrial
Location
in the
United States**

1 Introduction

This book presents the results of a study performed by Charles River Associates Incorporated for the Economic Development Administration to obtain long-term forecasts of economic growth in each of the 3,097 counties in the contiguous United States.[1] In particular, the goal was to develop a model or set of models of each area's industrial structure. Each county's future industrial structure could then be forecast based on the level and mix of its present industry and a limited number of relevant, easily obtainable socioeconomic variables.

Absolutely precise predictions of industrial activity for an individual county cannot be expected from such a study. Its principal contribution should be viewed as providing an analysis of the factors that cause, or are associated with, industrial location decisions and economic growth in small geographic and economic areas. In addition, the forecasts themselves can be useful for policy decisions. Predicted changes in an area's industrial activity, for example, together with information on its existing public facilities, can be used when attempting to determine whether additional public investment is reasonable in light of expected economic growth. In the case of a given locality, a detailed examination of its specific industrial structure will usually be more accurate than predictions from historical data; however, good predictive models are useful in comparing areas and general trends as part of the decision process.

When utilizing and interpreting the results of statistical models, the user must constantly keep in mind the facts that such models are based on historical data and that they are, by necessity, oversimplified descriptions of a highly complex process. While their aggregate predictions may be reliable, this does not imply that a detailed prediction for a single industry in a single locality will necessarily be realized. This fact does not impair the usefulness of this study as long as users do not attempt to make it imply more than the limitations of the data and the techniques of statistical inference will permit.

The following chapter reviews existing techniques of industrial location forecasting, describing their strengths and weaknesses. Chapter 3 describes in detail the general model developed to analyze industrial location, as well as presenting special techniques for dealing with industries that do not fit the general pattern. Chapter 4 describes the treatment of special problems of the model arising both from data limitation and

---

[1] Charles River Associates, *Area Employment Prediction to Determine Public Facilities Requirements,* prepared for U.S. Department of Commerce, Economic Development Administration, under contract C-315-65, Cambridge, Mass., January 1968.

1

statistical considerations. Chapter 5 describes the data available for analysis, the data actually used and the criteria used for their selection, and the estimation techniques. Chapter 6 contains a description of the equations that were estimated and a discussion and interpretation of projections made using these equations.

2

Existing Techniques for Interregional Forecasting of Economic Activity

Introduction

The basic objective of this study was interpreted to be to develop forecasts of employment by major industry groups for each county. Unfortunately, a search of the literature failed to reveal any techniques that would be directly useable for projecting employment by industry by county. A number of approaches — such as base theory (multiplier analysis), regional input–output, linear programming, and location analysis — were studied. But upon examination all these approaches were found to be inadequate.

Since there are a number of adequate summaries of techniques of regional analysis, no attempt will be made here to present an exhaustive treatment of all possible techniques.[1] However, an outline of the principal techniques and the reasons for rejecting each will be presented. Several techniques of regional analyses can be rejected because they either are techniques of describing data or are theories with little or no quantifiable content.

Flow Analysis

An example of the data-describing technique is flow analysis, which merely presents data in a form that is easy to read. The objectives of this study, of course, go beyond mere description of past industrial structure. Flow analysis usually involves drawing maps of the region to be analyzed (i.e., state or county) and indicating with the use of arrows or some other pictorial technique the destination and origin of products leaving and entering the region. Such "analysis" has little analytical content. Another device used by flow analysis is the location quotient, which compares a region's percentage share of a particular activity with its percentage share of a basic aggregate, such as income, value added, population, and area. The location quotient also is nothing more than a descriptive device, and its use may give rise to more confusion than understanding of causal forces. The weakness of its empirical use is illustrated in the following

---

[1] A brief summary is presented in Robert G. Spiegelman, *Review of Techniques of Regional Analysis with Particular Emphasis on Applicability of These Techniques to Regional Problems*, (Menlo Park, California: Stanford Research Institute, June 1962). A more comprehensive treatment is given in Walter Isard, *Methods of Regional Analysis: An Introduction to Regional Science* (Cambridge, Massachusetts: The M.I.T. Press, 1960).

statement: "We find in the regional literature suggestions that those industries with location quotients greater than unity represent the areas of strength within a region and ought therefore to be further developed; and, in somewhat contradictory fashion, that those industries with location quotients less than unity ought to be encouraged in order to reduce the drain of imports."[2]

Population and Industry Distribution
Comparisons

Benjamin Chinitz and Raymond Vernon have published a technique which, although still in the descriptive realm, offers considerable insight into industrial location.[3] Chinitz and Vernon analyzed geographic shifts of industries using data from the *Census of Manufactures* for 1939 and 1954 and found a "marked convergence in the ratio of manufacturing employment to population among the different regions of the country toward some common national ratios."[4] This trend was discovered in 90 of the 119 industries studied by calculating an index of concentration described as follows:

For each year, we compared the industry's employment distribution with the distribution of population among the major areas of the country. Then we calculated how many workers in the industry would have to be shifted in order to achieve a proportionate distribution of employment among the country's areas identical to the proportionate distribution of population. Finally, we expressed the number that would have to be shifted in the industry as a proportion of total national employment in the industry.[5]

The analysis of Chinitz and Vernon can be differentiated from the descriptive techniques in that they have attempted to find the causes of changes in their index. However, Chinitz and Vernon use a case study and anecdotal approach and their technique per se is consequently not applicable to our project, which requires a uniform and consistent statistical procedure that can be applied to all 3,000 counties of the United States. Furthermore, many of their statistical conclusions seem to be based on zero-order correlations—that is, the statistical correlations they compute do not take other simultaneous influences into account. However, the following findings are still useful as background material:
  1. The industries which grew fastest also moved fastest to conformity

---

[2] *Ibid.,* p. 525.

[3] Benjamin Chinitz and Raymond Vernon, "Changing Forces in Industrial Location," *Harvard Business Review* (January–February, 1960).

[4] *Ibid.,* p. 127.

[5] *Ibid.,* p. 129.

with the distribution of population; in other words, faster growing industries tend to be more decentralized relative to population.

2. One of the principal explanations for decentralization is lower transport costs; insofar as freight-cost data were available, they were positively correlated with a decline in concentration of an industry. That is,
industries with higher freight costs relative to other industries tended to
be the industries which had the highest rates of decline in the index of
concentration used by Chinitz and Vernon.

3. Another factor favoring decentralization is the increasing tendency
for plants to use already processed materials. Thus, availability of raw
materials has become less important as a factor determining plant
location.

4. The motor vehicle has decreased the cost of transport in a manner
that promotes the decentralization of industry. For example, trucking has
reduced the cost of shipping in small lots relative to the cost of shipping
in large lots. Chinitz and Vernon, however, point out that three recent
developments may have effects in the opposite direction: "the spread of
coordinated services such as 'piggy-back' and 'fishy-back;' the growing
use of air freight; and the prospective reorientation of the railroad rate
structure."[6]

5. Chinitz and Vernon argue that there is a growing availability of
skills in rural areas, largely as a result of transportation innovations and
greater industrial experience. The increased decentralization in availability of skills is thus another factor favoring decentralization of industries.

6. Another related factor is the fact that rural areas now can—and, according to Chinitz and Vernon, frequently do—provide facilities to industry on a competitive basis, partly because of the wider market areas of
existing facilities (such as trucking depots).

Chintiz and Vernon reason that industries are no longer tied down to
historical locations and to sources of raw materials and that economies
of agglomeration and of scale may not be as important as they have been
in the past. Changes in industrial location are much more possible now
than they have been in the past, and it thus becomes much more important
to identify those factors which make one county a more likely locale for
industrial expansion than another.

Industrial Location Theory

The other class of techniques that can be rejected consists of theoretical
studies of location which disregard quantification. Location theory may
in the long run lead to important conclusions for empirical analysis, but

[6]*Ibid.*

at the present it is inappropriate for projects such as the one described in this study. Location theory analyzes the location of firms by studying the comparative costs of different firms. Thus, location theory attempts to answer the following type of question: Given several sources of raw materials and several markets, where will a firm locate? The analysis can be complicated by varying the processing and transfer costs at various locations. A summary of the literature on location theory would be out of place in this study because location theory not only has little empirical content, but offers very unsurprising theoretical conclusions such as, "long-run competitive equilibrium in a space economy is the same as in a nonspace economy; that is, firms will produce where marginal cost equals marginal revenue and average cost equals price."[7] Location theory tends to be abstract and usually concerns itself with ideal worlds in which only a few variables are important in location decisions, whereas we must analyze industrial growth in the real world with all of its complications. Furthermore, even if location analysis did offer a rigorous and complete analysis of industrial growth, it would be useless for our project since it requires information which is simply not available. To apply location theory, at a minimum one would need a complete matrix of transport costs to and from every county for every different product, a matrix of processing costs at each county for every product, and a knowledge of the demand function for every product in every county. Location theory may thus be applicable if one intended to study intensively one small industry producing a well-defined product with known processing and transportation costs, but application of the theory on a universal basis is hopeless at present.

Base Theory

A technique that has found wide application is base theory, which is little more than a straightforward application of Keynesian multiplier theory. The latter theory states that for a simple, nonspatial, timeless economy with consumption of one good, imports of one good, unemployment of factors of production, and constant marginal propensities to consume and import, the following functional relationship holds:

$$Y = \frac{A}{1 - c + m} \qquad (2.1)$$

where Y is income, c is the marginal propensity to consume domestic goods, m is the marginal propensity to import, and A is exogenous expenditure. Base theory accepts this crude model and postulates that

[7] Spiegelman, *op. cit.*, p. 19.

total regional income is proportional to exports, which are in effect assumed to be the only exogenous expenditure. It is usually postulated that the basic to nonbasic ratio of a region will be constant, where "basic" refers to export industries and "nonbasic" refers to local service industries. The empirical procedure usually consists of calculating the base/service ratio, projecting exports, and multiplying this projection by the above ratio.[8]

Economic base theory, while apparently straightforward and simple, is plagued with difficulties, both in theory and in practical application.

Many theoretical objections can be raised to base theory. The theory assumes that all relationships within the region's economy will remain constant over time, an obviously deficient assumption. Not only must the marginal propensity to consume and the marginal propensity to import remain constant for all goods, but input–output interrelationships among industries must be constant over time. Furthermore, the theory ignores investment and assumes that exports are the only autonomous activities in the economy. Even if the assumption of no exogenous investment were true, base theory has no place for such "invisible" incomes as interest payments from other regions. The most fundamental objection is that, far from assuming that the base/service ratio is constant, the purpose of regional economics should be to explain the magnitude of this ratio and to be able to project changes in the ratio.

Base analysis assumes that the only dynamic component of an economy is its exports, and that all activities within the economy are dependent on its exports. The validity of this assumption is not obvious — it obviously is not true of the world as a whole and it has little relevance for a largely self-sufficient economy like that of the United States. One may ask at what stage do exogenously determined exports become crucial, or if they ever become crucial. For example, changes in productivity of local non-export industries may be just as important for growth as changes in demand for a region's exports.

Base analysis also provides no mechanism for predicting changes in demand for exports of a region. It may be feasible to do an extensive study of the potential demand for the exports of one small region, but base theory provides no mechanism for determining exports of each region if all regions in an economic system are being considered simultaneously. In particular, one needs to examine the feedback effects which occur as a result of a region's exports — i.e., region A imports from region B, thereby increasing B's income through a Keynesian multiplier effect.

[8] Economic base studies have been performed for Madison, Wisconsin by John W. Alexander; for Copenhagen by L. Barford; for Cincinnati by the Cincinnati City Planning Commission; for Wichita by the Federal Reserve Bank of Kansas City; for Los Angeles County by George Hildebrand and Arthur Mace, Jr.; for Brockton, Massachusetts, Arlington, Virginia, and Evanston, Illinois by Homer Hoyt; and for Denver by the Denver Planning Commission.

B's increase in income, in turn, induces an increase in B's imports from A, which increases A's income, etc. One possible model for incorporating feedback effects might be similar to the following:

Using the Keynesian income identity,

$$Y_i = C_i + I_i + X_i - M_i, \qquad i = 1, ..., n \qquad (2.2)$$

where C_i is consumption of county i, I_i is investment of county i; X_i is exports of county i and M_i is imports of county i.

If we assume a linear relationship between income and imports, then X_i, the sum of imports from county i of all other counties, may be represented as follows:

$$X_i = \sum_{j=1}^{n} m_{ij} Y_j = m_{i1} Y_1 + \cdots + m_{in} Y_n, \qquad i = 1, ..., n \qquad (2.3)$$

where m_{ij} represents the marginal propensity to import of county j from county i and $m_{ii} = 0$. Furthermore,

$$M_i = \sum_{j=1}^{n} m_{ji} Y_i = m_{1i} Y_i + \cdots + m_{ni} Y_i, \qquad i = 1, ..., n \qquad (2.4)$$

The equations for all counties may then be presented as follows, assuming a constant marginal propensity to consume (c_i) in each county and an exogenous investment function:

$$Y_1 = c_1 Y_1 + I_1 + m_{11} Y_1 + \cdots + m_{1n} Y_n - m_{11} Y_1 - \cdots - m_{n1} Y_1 \qquad (2.5.1)$$

$$Y_n = c_n Y_n + I_n + m_{n1} Y_1 + \cdots + m_{nn} Y_n - m_{1n} Y_n - \cdots - m_{nn} Y_n \qquad (2.5.n)$$

Transposing terms,

$$Y_1(1 - c_1 + m_{21} + \cdots + m_{n1} \quad - m_{12} Y_2 - \cdots - m_{1n} Y_n \quad = I_1 \qquad (2.6.1)$$

$$Y_n(1 - c_n + m_{1n} + \cdots + m_{n-1,n}) - m_{n2} Y_2 - \cdots - m_{n-1,n} Y_{n-1} = I_n \qquad (2.6.n)$$

The system of simultaneous equations in (2.6.1)–(2.6.n) may be solved for $(Y_1, ..., Y_n)$ as a function of $(I_1, ..., I_n)$. This model is subject to many of the shortcomings of base theory, but improves simple base theory by taking into account the feedback effects of trade among the various regions of the economy. The multiregion model presented above also serves to emphasize the inability of standard base theory to explain the structure of trade among regions. Base theory essentially assumes that the vector $(I_1, ..., I_n)$ contains a zero for every element. In the multiregion model which incorporates every assumption of base theory and adds no new assumptions, making this assumption results in overdeterminacy; that is, the resulting system of equations $(2.6.1)–(2.6.n)$ has no nonzero solution.

Even if the theoretical objections to base theory are overcome, the application of the technique encounters formidable obstacles. One immediately encounters the problem of how to measure economic activity. Most applications have used employment as a measure of activity, mainly because employment data are the easiest data to obtain. However, employment is peculiarly unsuited to the application of base theory, since one must adjust for changes in productivity between the service sector (which produces goods for domestic consumption) and the export sector. The best measure is probably value added, but data on value added are usually not available.

The researcher encounters an even greater difficulty when he tries to distinguish basic activities from nonbasic activities. In the first place, it is not clear how one should handle firms which produce both for export and for local consumption. Presumably, the firm's employment should be allocated between the basic and the service sectors according to the proportion of production that is sold in other regions. Information of this nature, however, is not available unless the researcher conducts a firm-to-firm survey. Such a survey would be a huge operation even in a small region, and it would be impossible to perform on a national basis.

A further problem presenting theoretical as well as practical difficulties arises when one considers the interdependencies inherent in a modern economy. For example, how should one handle the local firm that sells to another local firm which in turn exports a finished product? To find the employment that is indirectly as well as directly related to exports one needs a complete input–output table. It is furthermore not entirely clear what degree of "directness" is required for a firm's employment to be termed basic, for if the underlying assumptions of base theory are accepted, then all local employment is ultimately indirectly related to exports. Quite apart from this difficulty, the input–output data that would be needed are not at present available for any local region.

**Regional Input–Output Analysis
and Linear Programming
Techniques**

Two additional techniques have occasionally been attempted in regional economic analysis: input–output and linear programming. Both are considerably more sophisticated than the techniques we have already analyzed, but both unfortunately possess difficulties of their own for interregional forecasting.

As explained in Chapter 3, for consistency, the forecasts of this study are integrated into a national input–output model. This model and the basic structure of input–output analysis are described in detail in Appendix A, and a repetition of that discussion would be redundant. Regional input–output analysis possesses all the theoretical and practical drawbacks of input–output analysis at the national level, in addition to a number of deficiencies of its own. For example, interregional input–output models are usually forced to assume constant coefficients of trade among regions. The assumption of constant trade coefficients is not terribly serious for a model of an economy such as that of the United States, as imports and exports of the United States each represent only about 3 percent of GNP. The "smaller" and more open a region becomes, however, the more serious becomes the problem of how to treat trade among regions. Wassily Leontief, in a well-known study assumes that there are two classes of economic goods: those whose outputs are determined regionally and those whose outputs are determined in a national model.[9] He first calculates the latter, distributes the predicted value to the regions in fixed proportions, and then calculates the outputs of regional goods. Such a model may not cause great inaccuracy when applied to broad regions which have relatively small interregional trade, but it becomes an exercise in futility when applied to regions as small as counties. In many counties almost all economic activity is concentrated in exports and imports; a model assuming constant trade coefficients for small regions assumes away what should be analyzed in the case of open economies: the determinants of the volume and composition of trade. Of greater relevance for our project, however, is the fact that data do not exist for the construction of county input–output tables.

Linear programming has the advantage that it permits the consideration of various sources of supply, with the level of each solved by the model. In general, linear programming will answer the following type of question: Given the quantity of the various scarce factors and the (linear) production functions for producing outputs, what is the most efficient method of allocating the scarce factors from the point of view of achieving a certain specified objective (i.e., maximizing profits, social welfare, employment, etc.)? Linear programming, while applicable to such problems as finding the optimum operation of a farm producing several outputs and using several inputs, is not a relevant technique for our purpose primarily because the data it requires are not available and because no operational interregional models have yet been formulated. Furthermore, linear programming is of little use for the limited objective of predicting employment; linear programming calculates the optimal allocation of resources, but it does not predict actual behavior.

[9] Wassily Leontief, *Studies in the Structure of the American Economy*. (New York: Oxford University Press, 1953).

Shift Analysis

In the brief review we have given above we have attempted to show why the formal regional economic models are not applicable to the problem of projecting employment by county. A number of less formal approaches are available, however, which may yield meaningful empirical projections, such as the "shift" method used by Fuchs, Ashby, Perloff, and others.[10]

In the shift method, the industrial growth of states is computed after an adjustment for the effects of industrial structure. That is, for a given state, "comparative growth, adjusted for industrial structure, shows what the comparative gain or loss would have been if all the other states had had an industrial structure comparable to the state in question. Comparative industrial structure shows what the comparative gain or loss would have been if each industry in the state had grown at its national rate."[11]

The exact meaning of these definitions requires further refinement. The actual formula Fuchs uses to compute "comparative gain or loss, all manufacturing, state s adjusted for industrial structure (percent)" appears as follows:

$$M = \frac{1}{2} \left(\frac{Y_{s\cdot} - \sum_i X_{si} \frac{Y_{\cdot i}}{X_{\cdot i}}}{Y_{s\cdot}} + \frac{\sum_i Y_{si} \frac{X_{\cdot i}}{Y_{\cdot i}} - X_{s\cdot}}{X_{s\cdot}} \right) \qquad (2.7)$$

where:

X_{si} = economic activity (e.g., employment) in initial year (e.g., 1929) of industry i in state s.

$X_{s\cdot}$ = economic activity in initial year (e.g., 1929) of all industries in state s.

$X_{\cdot i}$ = economic activity in initial year (e.g., 1929) of industry i in the United States.

$X_{\cdot\cdot}$ = economic activity in initial year (e.g., 1929) of all industries in the United States.

Y_{si}, $Y_{s\cdot}$, $Y_{\cdot i}$, and Y represent the economic activities in the terminal year (e.g., 1954).

The common-sense reasoning behind the formulation of equation (2.7) may be stated somewhat as follows: Given the percentage composition of manufacturing employment by industry in a state in the base year, the

---

[10] Victor R. Fuchs, *Changes in the Location of Manufacturing in the United States Since 1929* (New Haven: Yale University Press, 1962); Lowell D. Ashby, "Regional Change in a National Setting," *Staff Working Paper in Economics and Statistics, No. 7* (U.S. Dept. of Commerce, April 1964); Harvey S. Perloff, "How a Region Grows," *Supplementary Paper No. 17* (Committee for Economic Development, March 1963).

[11] Fuchs, *op. cit.*, p. 62.

growth that would occur if all industries already located in that state grew at their respective national rates is represented by the term

$$\sum_i X_{si} \frac{Y_{\cdot i}}{X_{\cdot i}}$$

This prediction represents the growth the state would have if no special factors peculiar to that state affected economic activity. The deviation of *actual* growth from the *predicted* growth is then measured by the term

$$Y_{s\cdot} - \sum_i X_{si} \frac{Y_{\cdot i}}{X_{\cdot i}}$$

This deviation is then expressed in percentage terms by dividing through by a base: in equation (2.7) the base is $Y_{s\cdot}$.

There are several statistical ambiguities inherent in Fuchs' definition. In the first place, there is no clear basis for choosing any one year as a base. As Fuchs states it, the "method of measuring the influence of industrial structure is not precise because it is based entirely on the structure of the initial year."[12] It is not apparent how this shortcoming could be overcome, because the choice of any one year or combination of years as the base could be criticized as artificial. Fuchs has attempted to partially adjust for this ambiguity by making his definition the average of two percentage deviations. The first deviation measurement we have described above; the second is the mirror image of the first, with the initial year used as a base. The artificiality inherent in choosing a base year is still present, however. The other principal ambiguity is that the choice of the denominator for deflation is arbitrary. For example, in equation (2.7) one may with equal justification divide by $Y_{s\cdot}$ instead of $X_{s\cdot}$. This latter ambiguity in definition is independent of the ambiguity inherent in choosing a base year.

The concept of "comparative industrial structure" in state s may be represented as follows:

$$N = \frac{1}{2}\left(\frac{\sum_i X_{si}\frac{Y_{\cdot i}}{X_{\cdot i}} - X_{s\cdot}\frac{Y_{\cdot\cdot}}{X_{\cdot\cdot}}}{\sum_i X_{si}\frac{Y_{\cdot i}}{X_{\cdot i}}} + \frac{Y_{s\cdot}\frac{X_{\cdot\cdot}}{Y_{\cdot\cdot}} - \sum_i Y_{si}\frac{X_{\cdot i}}{Y_{\cdot i}}}{\sum_i Y_{si}\frac{X_{\cdot i}}{Y_{\cdot i}}} \right) \qquad (2.8)$$

where the dots in place of subscripts indicate that the summation over the index has been performed. The principal use of this variable is to test

[12] *Ibid.*, p. 12.

whether a particular state has an industrial composition which is "favorable" to growth. Thus, starting in the base year, the employment that would occur if every industry grew at the national rate for that industry is measured by the term

$$\sum_i X_{si} \frac{Y_{\cdot i}}{X_{\cdot i}}$$

The manufacturing employment the state would have if all industries in the state grew at the national rate of growth of all manufacturing can then be measured by the term $X_{s.}(Y_{..}/X_{..})$. The latter calculated employment is subtracted from the former and the difference is then expressed in percentage terms, as follows:

$$\frac{\sum_i X_{si} \frac{Y_{\cdot i}}{X_{\cdot i}} - X_{s.} \frac{Y_{..}}{X_{..}}}{\sum_i X_{si} \frac{Y_{\cdot i}}{X_{\cdot i}}}$$

In the second term of equation (2.8) Fuchs again adjusts for the ambiguity of choosing a particular base year.

While Fuchs' technique yields some useful insights, its analytical relevance for our purposes is not clear. The shift approach is essentially a method of presenting the data in a form which is easy to digest. Fuchs, however, goes further than this and computes regressions with socioeconomic characteristics as independent variables and comparative growth of manufacturing (percent), adjusted, as the dependent variable.

The basic premise of the shift technique is that past industrial structure is of overwhelming importance and that this importance enters in a particular prespecified manner. If each industry in every county had the national rate of growth, or if deviations from the national growth rate were small and easily explainable, then a method of analysis which places major emphasis on shares of industrial growth would have great relevance. The data do not support such a conclusion. Fuchs himself states that

. . . the redistribution of manufacturing since 1929 has been primarily the result of area differentials in the growth of individual industries. Two important pieces of evidence support this conclusion. First, when the comparative gain or loss by division is divided into the portion attributable to the comparative gain or loss of individual industries and the portion attributable to differences in industrial structure, the former proves to be much larger. Second, the correlation between state comparative gain or loss of manufacturing, unadjusted, and comparative gain or loss, adjusted for industrial structure, is very high (Spearman's rho =

+.811), whereas there is no correlation between comparative gain or loss, unadjusted, and comparative industrial structure (Spearman's rho = +.033).[13]

In other words, Fuchs makes the interesting finding that there is little association between a state's unadjusted comparative growth and the proportion of high-growth industries that it has, where comparative gain or loss, all manufacturing, for state s in percent may be represented as follows:

$$\frac{Y_{s\cdot} - X_{s\cdot}\,\frac{Y_{\cdot\cdot}}{X_{\cdot\cdot}}}{Y_{s\cdot}}$$

Thus, the fact that a state has high-growth industries in the base year does not in general imply that its growth will be greater than average growth of manufacturing in the United States. Fuchs' results apparently are not a quirk of aggregation—thus, "adjustment for structure becomes more important the finer the detail, but the differences are not that great."[14]

Ashby has further discerned that recently there has been a "relative rise in the importance of competitive and a relative decline in the importance of industrial mix effects in local areas."[15] In Fuchs' notation, the industrial mix effect can be defined as

$$\sum_i X_{si}\,\frac{Y_{\cdot i}}{X_{\cdot i}} - X_{s\cdot}\,\frac{Y_{\cdot\cdot}}{X_{\cdot\cdot}}$$

and the competitive effect as

$$Y_{s\cdot} - \sum_i X_{si}\,\frac{Y_{\cdot i}}{X_{\cdot i}}$$

Thus, Ashby's formulation corresponds almost exactly to Fuchs' "comparative gain, adjusted for industrial structure" formulation, except that Ashby does not express his computations in percentage terms and only presents his results using one base year instead of an average of the results using two base years.

Ashby attributes the rise in the importance of the competitive effect to two factors: "The post-war slack has given various local areas the opportunity to expand industrial employments at widely divergent rates . . . and the importance of industry mix effects appears to have been undermined to some extent by an increase in the homogeneity of local

[13] Ibid.
[14] Ibid., p. 80.
[15] Ashby, op. cit., p. 24.

15

industrial structure."[16] Thus, not only is past industry mix not of overwhelming importance, but this factor is becoming increasingly less important.

Fuchs' regression equations assume that the functional relationship of industrial employment variables to socioeconomic variables is of the following form:

$$M = \alpha + \beta_1 Y_1^i + \beta_2 Y_2^i + \cdots + \beta_n Y_n^i \qquad (2.9)$$

where M is "comparative gain or loss, all manufacturing, state s adjusted for industrial structure (percent)" and Y_1^i through Y_n^i are n socioeconomic variables in state i in period 1. The model implied in equation (2.9) requires further analysis. If the variable M is expressed in percentage form, and the fact that it is an average over two base years is ignored, M can be defined as follows:

$$M = \frac{Y_{s\cdot} - \sum_i X_{si} \dfrac{Y_{\cdot i}}{X_{\cdot i}}}{Y_{s\cdot}} \qquad (2.10)$$

Equation (2.9) then becomes

$$Y_{s\cdot} = \alpha Y_{s\cdot} + \beta_1 Y_1^i Y_{s\cdot} + \beta_2 Y_2^i Y_{s\cdot} + \cdots + \beta_n Y_n^i Y_{s\cdot} + \sum_i X_{si} \frac{Y_{\cdot i}}{X_{\cdot i}} \qquad (2.11)$$

We can discern no economic justification for such a model. If we use as the dependent variable the Ashby competitive effect, we obtain a more defensible model:

$$Y_{s\cdot} - \sum_i X_{si} \frac{Y_{\cdot i}}{X_{\cdot i}} = \alpha + \beta_1 Y_1^i + \beta_2 Y_2^i + \cdots + \beta_n Y_n^i \qquad (2.12)$$

Completely aside from possible errors in Fuchs' specification of functional forms and in choice of explanatory variables, a basic shortcoming of the shift analysis in this form is that it constrains the coefficient of the constructed variable

$$\sum_i X_{si} \frac{Y_{\cdot i}}{X_{\cdot i}}$$

to be one. That is, the formulation of equation (2.12) is equivalent to the following formulation, with the coefficient γ constrained to equal 1:

[16] Ibid., p. 27.

$$Y_{s.} = \alpha + \beta_1 Y_1^i + \beta_2 Y_2^i + \cdots + \beta_n Y_n^i + \gamma \sum_i X_{si} \frac{Y_{\cdot i}}{X_{\cdot i}} \qquad (2.13)$$

There can be no question that the degree and structure of past industrial activity in a region will, for a number of reasons which will be discussed below, have a major influence on the degree and structure of future industrial activity, but the magnitude and statistical significance of this influence should be one of the objects of research, not one of the assumptions of research.

Fuchs also ignores the difficult problem of identifying the simultaneous interplay of forces inherent in regional economics. This shortcoming cannot be attributed solely to his model, since the problem is exceedingly difficult to solve; in fact, there has been virtually no published empirical research in regional economics that considers the problem.

To understand the bias that arises from failing to consider the problem of simultaneity, a basic conception of the theory of estimation of simultaneous equations is needed. The simplest example of a simultaneous system is that involving the supply and demand for a commodity (such as, for example, labor or employment). Suppose the system of equations describing supply and demand for labor were the following:

$$D = a - bP + u \qquad (2.14)$$

$$S = c + dP + eW + v \qquad (2.15)$$

$$S = D \qquad (2.16)$$

In these equations, D represents demand, P represents price, S represents supply, and W represents an exogenous variable such as "amount of rainfall." The first equation is the demand function, the second is the supply function, and the third is a market equilibrium condition, stating that all observed price-quantity points represent points of equality of price and demand. A representation of the system is shown in Figure 2–1A. As indicated there, the price–quantity points trace out the demand curve. For a case such as this there exist consistent estimates of the demand curve. However, suppose instead that demand were a function of income in addition to price. In that case, the equilibrium points indicated in Figure 2–1B would be observed. A regression of Q on P in this case does not yield an unbiased estimate of either the demand function or the supply function.

As the above example indicates, correct specification of the structural relationships underlying observed data is extremely important. If the structural simultaneous model is specified, statistical estimation techniques are available which will yield asymptotically unbiased estimates

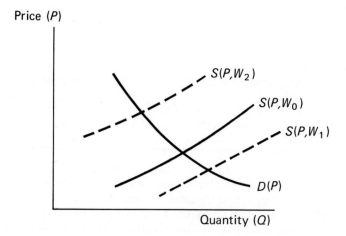

Figure 2–1A

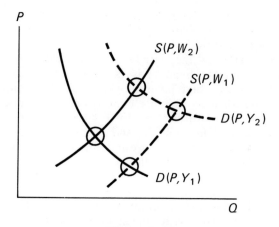

Figure 2–1B

of all equations of the system that are "statistically identified." In the example given above, the demand equation is identified, while the supply equation is not.

The problem of simultaneity is basic to regional economics as almost all the variables that one observes represent the outcomes of simultaneous interactions. Thus, Fuchs in his model postulates that growth in manufacturing is related to the following variables:[17]

---

[17] Fuchs, *op. cit.*, p. 87.

1. Consumer demand	6. Wage levels
2. Raw materials	7. Extent of unionization
3. Taxes	8. Space (land)
4. Foreign trade shifts	9. Climate
5. Federal government dispersal policy	10. Initial economic activity[18]

To these variables many other related variables may be added which measure the desirability of an area for industry, such as skill structure, external economies arising from the preexistence of industrialization, and such variables as attractiveness of the residential areas and the quality of cultural life which are proxies for the ability of the area to attract the managerial talent required by industry.

It may be noted that many of the variables and postulated relationships are recursive in nature—that is, they may be related to economic activity in the past, and may, in turn, affect economic activity in the future. For example, an area may have a favorable skill structure because it was industrialized in the past. This skill structure in turn may help cause future favorable increases in industrial activity. As one would expect, the statistical difficulties of disentangling the true causal relationships are great indeed.

In addition, many of the variables are endogenous. For example, suppose the reasonable hypothesis is made that industries locate in areas with low wages and labor moves into areas with high wages. It is not possible then to estimate employment as a function of wages without independent information. In Figure 2–2 we observe point *1* in 1950 and point *2* in 1960. D_1 and D_2 represent the demand functions for labor, and S_1 and S_2 represent the supply functions for labor in 1950 and 1960, respectively. Between 1950 and 1960 both the demand and the supply functions have shifted up. It is clear by examining Figure 2–2 that statistically relating employment to wages yields neither the demand function nor the supply function of labor. A similar problem arises with almost every other variable in regional analysis.

Fuchs makes no attempt to correct for simultaneity, although he presents evidence that the problem is pervasive in regional economics. For example, he quotes Creamer as stating that with respect to shifts of U.S. industries from 1929 to 1937, "the most common reason found was market considerations."[19] He then quotes Perloff, Dunn, Lampard, and Muth as stating that "shifts in final markets . . . have been closely related with

---

[18]The "catching up hypothesis" maintains that the states that have been experiencing rapid growth in recent years have been doing so primarily because of the low levels from which they began.

[19]*Ibid.*

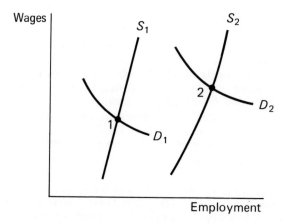

Wages

S_1

S_2

D_1

D_2

1

2

Employment

Figure 2–2

major shifts in manufacturing employment."[20] Again, he states that demand has not been a major determinant of locational change, partly because "a significant portion of the changes in demand that did occur should be considered a *result* of the redistribution of manufacturing."[21] He also recognizes that the "growth of population and income in California was in response to employment opportunities rather than the reverse."[22]

Perloff and Dodds, who also do not specifically examine the problem of simultaneity, presents arguments which implicitly assume simultaneity. For example, they state that "the importance of intermediate inputs, such as partially manufactured products, or markets, and of scale economies suggests why the *existing* distribution of population and economic activities among and within the region is itself a factor in the differing patterns of regions' growth."[23]

As explained above, the dependent variables used in Fuchs' shift technique do not appear to be meaningful for our purposes. Another shortcoming of Fuchs' model is his failure to consider the simultaneity problem, although it is difficult to fault him for this, for it would be exceedingly difficult to find a satisfactory solution to this problem. Although we have not found Fuchs' model to be completely satisfactory, his formulation is sufficiently similar to ours to warrant an examination of his results. In the regression analysis described above, the first five variables were

---

[20] *Ibid.*, p. 88.

[21] *Ibid.*, p. 62.

[22] *Ibid.*, p. 163.

[23] Perloff, *op. cit.*, p. 26.

eliminated because of lack of data or because of a priori arguments that they would not prove to be significantly related to change in employment. Of the variables studied, the following were found to be significantly related to change in employment: the relative extent of unionization, climate (deviation of mean temperature from 65°), and population density (population per square mile). Fuchs concludes that while for manufacturing as a whole the degree of unionization in a state is an important explanatory variable, interstate differences in the supply of unskilled labor are most important in low-wage, labor-intensive industries.

Fuchs also attempted to find which industry characteristics are related to industry differences in mobility. In Fuchs' analysis,

... mobility is defined as the extent to which an industry is located differently in one year as compared with an earlier year. If every state, for example, had the same percentage of industry x in period two as it had in period one, our measure would show zero interstate mobility. At the other extreme, an industry would record an interstate mobility of 100 percent if it were located in entirely different states in period two compared with period one. The measure of mobility, or percentage "shift," is the sum of the gain (in percent) of all states that increased their percentage share of a given industry between two dates.[24]

It should be noted that this definition "is not a synonym for physical movement. . . . An industry's geographical distribution changes more often through differential growth than through physical movement of plants or firms. Mobility measures the extent of this change, regardless of how it occurred."[25]

Fuchs tested the significance of the following industry variables as determinants of mobility: rate of growth; horsepower per worker; the ratio of wages to value added; concentration of ownership; average wages per production worker man-hour; percent of total employment in multiunit establishments; percent of value added produced in small companies; geographical concentration (scatter); number of workers per establishment; rate of change of wages; industry size; and an industry specialization ratio. In a multiple regression analysis the following variables were found to be statistically significant: rate of growth (positively correlated with mobility); average wage (negatively correlated); and concentration (positively correlated), with a peaking of mobility at the middle ranges of concentration. Somewhat surprisingly, Fuchs found that industries with high fixed costs were not less mobile, ceteris paribus, than industries with low fixed costs; furthermore, the market-oriented industries, taken individually, tended to be less mobile than other industries.

---

[24] Fuchs, *op. cit.*, p. 105.
[25] *Ibid.*

3 Formulation of the Model

Introduction

In the above critique of the various techniques which have been used or advocated for regional economic models, we have touched on many of the problems involved in constructing our own model. While it is theoretically possible to formulate a model which integrates the regional and the national economies, empirical implementation of such a model is very difficult.

The model presented below is designed to obtain ten-year projections of employment by industry for every county in the contiguous United States. Estimated equations relating 1960 employment to 1950 socioeconomic data were used to calculate expected 1970 employment from 1960 socioeconomic data. To correct for the fact that there was no guarantee that the aggregated county projections for 1970 would be consistent with known input-output relationships among industries or that the projected labor requirements for the country would equal the 1970 labor supply, our results were integrated with the projections of a national interindustry model constructed by Clopper Almon. Our county projections for each industry were scaled to make the aggregate estimate of employment for each industry equal to Almon's employment projection for the corresponding industry. The exact scaling procedures are described below.

Formulation of the General Model

We propose the following "structural" equations for the determinants of employment in industry j in country i:

$$E_{1,t}^{ij} = f_1^{ij}(\bar{Q}_t^i, P_t^i, V_{t-1}^i), \qquad j = 1, ..., f \tag{3.1}$$

$$E_{2,t}^{ij} = f_2^{ij}(\bar{Q}_t^i, P_t^i, E_{2,t-1}^{ij}, V_{t-1}^i), \qquad j = 1, ..., f \tag{3.2}$$

$$E_t^{ij} = E_{1,t}^{ij} + E_{2,t}^{ij}, \qquad j = 1, ..., f \tag{3.3}$$

$$P_t^i = h(\bar{E}_{t-1}^i, \bar{Q}_{t-1}^i, ..., \bar{E}_{t-s}^i, \bar{Q}_{t-s}^i) \tag{3.4}$$

$$V_{t-1}^i = g(\bar{E}_{t-1}^i, ..., \bar{E}_{t-n}^i) \tag{3.5}$$

$$Q_{1,t}^i = g^1(\bar{Q}_{t-1}^i, V_{t-1}^i) \tag{3.6.1}$$

$$\begin{matrix} \cdot & \cdot & \cdot & \cdot & & \cdot \\ \cdot & \cdot & \cdot & \vdots & & \cdot \\ \cdot & \cdot & \cdot & \cdot & & \cdot \end{matrix}$$

$$Q_{m,t}^i = g^m(\bar{Q}_{t-1}^i, V_{t-1}^i) \tag{3.6.m}$$

21

where

$E^{ij}_{1,t}$ = employment in period t for county i, industry j, in new establishments not present in period $t-1$;

$E^{ij}_{2,t}$ = employment in period t for county i, industry j, in previously established firms;

P^i_t = labor force (or "size") variable for county i in period t;

V^i_t = industrial structure indicator for county i in period t;

$\bar{E}^i_t = (E^{i1}_t, ..., E^{if}_t)$ = an f-dimensional vector of employment rates by industry in county i in period t;

and

$\bar{Q}^i_t = (Q^i_{1,t}, ..., Q^i_{m,t})$ = an m-dimensional vector of socioeconomic characteristics of county i in period t.

The model is recursive in form with autocorrelation of the error terms likely. The recursiveness may be a misspecification if some of the socioeconomic variables are related to *current* economic activity and other *current* socioeconomic variables. For example, variables such as the wage level are probably dependent on both current and lagged (predetermined) variables.

Equation (3.1) states that current employment in county i resulting from new firms in an industry ($E^{ij}_{1,t}$) is a function of the vector of socioeconomic variables, $\bar{Q}^i_t$, "(population) size" of the county, P^i_t, and the industrial structure of period $t-1$, V^i_{t-1}. Equation (3.2) states that current employment in firms already established in the county, $E^{ij}_{2,t}$ is a function of $\bar{Q}^i_t$, P^i_t, V^i_{t-1}, and lagged employment in those firms, $E^i_{2,t-1}$. Equation (3.3) is an identity defining total employment in county i in industry j. Equation (3.4) states that the size of the labor force is a function of past employment and socioeconomic variables in years $t-1$ through $t-s$. Equation (3.5) specifies the industrial structure to be a function of the vector of lagged employments. Equations (3.6.1) through (3.6. m) state that the vector of socioeconomic variables ($\bar{Q}^i_t$) describing the county is in turn a function of $\bar{Q}^i_{t-1}$ and the industrial structure of period $t-1$, V^i_{t-1}.

The first two equations are essentially reduced-form relationships between the derived demand for labor and the determinants of industrial location. Alternatively, the equations may be viewed as specifying determinants of industrial location with employment serving as a proxy for activity or production rates. For this latter view to be appropriate we must assume a constant output-labor ratio within an industry.

Current employment in a given county can be partitioned into that arising from employment generated by new plants [equation (3.1)] and that arising from employment in old plants [equation (3.2)]. The form of equation (3.1) may not be very similar to that of equation (3.2). The forces leading to establishment of a plant are not the same as those leading to expansion or contraction of an old plant.

In the first case, we are concerned with location theory — why does a new firm locate in County A instead of County B? If we postulate rational profit-maximizing behavior to firms, the sole criterion of location is long-run maximization of profits. Under this assumption all we need to consider are costs (of manufacturing, transporting, marketing, etc.) in order to determine location. Unfortunately, the cost data required for such predictions are not available. The data required go far beyond such conventional items as freight and power costs for a region. For example, the socioeconomic characteristics of a region can be very important in determining costs. A highly educated, skilled labor force may enable firms to produce at a lower cost even though they must pay higher wages; or the physical, social, and cultural attractiveness of an area may be an important determinant of the cost of obtaining efficient managerial talent.

Costs of production may also be lowered as a result of economies of scale and of external economies, quite apart from the natural resources of a region. For example, the study of the New York metropolitan area by Vernon highlights the role of agglomeration economies for supporting the growth of New York, an area that is otherwise poorly endowed.[1] The Los Angeles study by Pegrum also confirms the fact that agglomeration factors are quite significant for location decisions.[2]

In equation (3.1) the variables V_{t-1} and P_t represent some of these agglomeration economies. The size variable, P_t, also serves as a scaling factor. If two counties can be described by the same socioeconomic vector and have the same industrial structure, the size variable will ensure a prediction of greater employment in the county which has a larger initial labor force.

Equation (3.2) relates employment in already established plants to the characteristics of the county. In addition to lagged employment, the same variables (socioeconomic characteristics, industrial structure, and size) appear in equation (3.2) as in equation (3.1), but there is no reason a priori to expect the coefficients to be the same. The presence of lagged industry employment in equation (3.2) basically reflects inertia and economies of agglomeration. Because the costs of a locational change are not trivial, a plant that does not move, even though de novo other counties might be superior locations, may be acting completely rationally. Similarly, an establishment may not relocate until absolutely forced to do so, although relocation might be economically rational even with

[1] Raymond Vernon, *Metropolis 1985: An Interpretation of the New York Metropolitan Region Study* (Volume 9 of the New York Metropolitan Region Study, Harvard University Press, Cambridge, Massachusetts, 1960).

[2] Dudley Frank Pegrum, *Urban Transport and the Location of Industry in Metropolitan Los Angeles* (Los Angeles Bureau of Business and Economic Research, 1963).

moving costs included. In this case, lagged employment is a surrogate for decision-making inertia. The lagged employment variable also serves as a proxy for the cumulative effect of past values of socioeconomic variables and the unique characteristics making a county a desirable place to locate that have not been accounted for by other variables in the regression. Finally, the lagged employment variable may be regarded as a proxy for an industry's viability in a county.

Direct estimation of equations (3.1) through (3.6) raises a number of problems. First, the data for some independent variables are not available, either because they haven't been collected or because the variables are by nature unquantifiable. A major example of this problem is the lack of data concerning social overhead capital. Second, the data required to segregate employment in new plants from employment in old plants are not available except in cases where an industry is represented in a county for the first time; as a result we are forced to aggregate equations (3.1) and (3.2). Furthermore, it would be extremely difficult to construct an adequate formal model to determine the size of the labor force by county [equation (3.4)], the previously existing industrial structure [equation (3.5)], or the vector of socioeconomic characteristics of each county [equations (3.6.1)–(3.6.m)]. Consequently, we simplified the approach by substituting equations (3.5) and (3.6.1)–(3.6.m) into the two employment equations and then aggregating to form the following "partially reduced-form" equation:

$$E_t^{ij} = h^j(\bar{Q}_{t-1}^i, P_t^i, E_{t-1}^{ij}), \qquad j = 1, ..., f \tag{3.7}$$

Because of the prohibitive cost involved, we did not attempt to deal with autocorrelation of the error terms. Although autocorrelation would not affect the accuracy of predictions, the presence of a lagged dependent variable would result in estimation of individual coefficients being biased. Because the structural model is rather loosely specified, and because P_t is not an exogenous variable, equation (3.7) is not an ideal form for estimation. However, data are available for the variables included in the specification; the direct inclusion of P_t^i removed the need for data lagged more than one period.

The relationships specified in equations (3.1) through (3.7) are almost certainly not linear. To assert linearity would be to assert, for example, that the absolute effect on employment of a one-year increase in average years of schooling is constant for all counties, independent of all other variables, including such "size" variables as lagged employment or total labor force.

As an alternative to linearity, we have specified the model in the following form:

$$\ln E_t^{ij} = a_j + b_{1j}Q_{1,t}^i + \cdots + b_{mj}Q_{m,t}^i + \gamma_j \ln P_t^i + \mu_j \ln E_{t-1}^{ij} + \ln \epsilon_1^{ij},$$
$$j = 1, ..., f \tag{3.8}$$

$$Q^i_{1,t} = c_1 + d_{11}Q^i_{1,t-1} + \cdots + d_{1m}Q^i_{m,t-1} + \rho_1 V^i_{t-1} + \epsilon^i_{11} \tag{3.9.1}$$

. . . .

$$Q^t_{m,t} = c_m + d_{m1}Q^i_{1,t-1} + \cdots + d_{m,m}Q^i_{m,t-1} + \rho_m V^i_{t-1} + \epsilon^i_{1m} \tag{3.9.m}$$

$$\ln E^{ij}_t = \alpha_j + \beta_{ij}Q^i_{1,t-1} + \cdots + \beta_{mj}Q^i_{m,t-1} + C_j V^i_{t-1} + \gamma_j \ln P^i_t$$
$$+ \mu_j \ln E^{ij}_{t-1} + \ln \epsilon^{ij}_1 + \beta_{1j}\epsilon^i_{11} + \cdots + \beta_{mj}\epsilon^i_{1mj}, \qquad j = 1,...,f \tag{3.10}$$

The variables ϵ_1 and ϵ_{11} through ϵ_{1m} are error terms of equations (3.8) and (3.9) respectively; ln indicates a natural logarithm.

Rewriting the model in nonlogarithmic form, we have

$$E^{ij}_t = (E^{ij}_{t-1})^{\mu_j}(P^i_t)^{\gamma_j} \exp\{a_j + b_{1j}Q^i_{1,t} + \cdots$$
$$+ b_{mj}Q^i_{m,t}\}\epsilon^{ij}_1, \qquad j = 1,...,f \tag{3.8.1}$$

$$E^{ij}_t = (E^{ij}_{t-1})^{\mu_j}(P^i_t)^{\gamma_j} \exp\{\alpha_j + \beta_{1j}Q^i_{1,t-1} + \cdots$$
$$+ \beta_{mj}Q^i_{m,t-1} + C_j V^i_{t-1} + b_{ij}\epsilon^i_{11} + \cdots + b_{mj}\epsilon^i_{1m}\}\epsilon^{ij}_1, \qquad j = 1,...,f \tag{3.10.1}$$

The socioeconomic variables in equation (3.10.1) could be in multiplicative form also, but the chosen exponential form has the advantage of avoiding the mathematical difficulties that arise when one or more of the socioeconomic variables has a zero value in one or more counties. In the exponential–multiplicative model this situation is innocuous but in a pure multiplicative model a zero value anywhere in the Q vector would produce a zero employment prediction.

The Aggregation Problem

A difficulty with any nonlinear model is that linear aggregation of nonlinear functions destroys the functional form of the model unless very special assumptions are made. If the true relation is nonlinear, we have no recourse other than fitting what we believe is the true relationship to the data. If μ is close to one [see equation (3.10)], the bias from aggregation over industries will not be very serious, and if μ and γ are close to one the bias from aggregation over counties will not be serious. If the values of μ and γ are substantially different from one, care must be taken to avoid misuse of the reported equations. If, for example, μ and γ in a particular equation were substantially greater than one and the county equations were applied to states, the projected employments would be absurdly large.

If we have reason to believe that one particular size unit is relevant, to avoid aggregation bias we would have to estimate the equations for regions of that size. The aggregation problem is therefore directly related to the correct choice of the range and domain of the function estimated.

As happens so often in empirical studies, we are constrained to examine economic relationships with data which probably are for areas different from those relevant to the functions being considered. The two area classifications we could have used for our study are state economic areas and counties. Data do exist for other small-area classifications, such as metropolitan areas, but the data do not exist on a national scale in a consistent, mutually exclusive, and exhaustive form. Given the lack of information on the relevant functional area, and because counties were the most relevant units for EDA policy, we chose the county as the basic unit of analysis.[3]

In theory, a sound allocation model should account for both the choice of the function and of the observations, in this case the units for which the observations are defined. Two areas which are functionally relevant to a business are its source of supply and its market. In theory the location of the business depends upon which of these two areas is more restrictive in its influence. For instance, retail outlets and personal service industries locate as close as possible to the market they are trying to serve. In industries that depend heavily upon natural resources, it may be cheaper to process goods near the supply source than to ship raw materials to market areas for processing.

The dependence of many industries on local markets or sources of supply apparently has declined over time. This is primarily because transportation costs are lower relative to the value of output than they were in the past; industry is much less reliant on naturally occurring raw materials, and markets are less concentrated today than they were in the past.

Nevertheless, the concept of a "restriction area" is still important in many cases. Such restriction areas vary greatly in size from industry to industry. For the drug store, the area is a neighborhood. For the regional assembly plant of an automobile manufacturer, the restriction area may be several states.

Of course, there may be little relationship between "areas" of economic influence and physical area. The restriction area for a firm may be physically small where the population is dense but much larger in sparsely settled areas. For many industries it would be impossible to choose a constant physical area for measurement which would be appropriate throughout the United States.

In fact, we do not have a consistent unit throughout the United States. The size and complexion of counties vary enormously throughout the nation, and there is no apparent relationship—nor should we expect a relationship—between this variation and the variations we might expect to occur over the restriction areas appropriate to particular industries.

Because of the importance of area definition and because of our in-

---

[3] It should be recalled that this study was initially done under contract to the Economic Development Administration.

ability to identify the appropriate areas for observation, statistical analysis must be carried out with variables that are invariant to area definition. In equations (3.8) through (3.10) we have compromised by using Q variables that are scale free and nonadditive while maintaining scale effects with variables E_t, E_{t-1}, and P_t. Alternatively, we could make all variables scale free by eliminating P_t and dividing equation (3.10.1) by E^μ. Unfortunately, this procedure may involve a considerable misspecification, as it requires the elimination of a variable and the prespecification of μ (although the problem of aggregation would be sidestepped). A special case of this would be to specify μ to be equal to one; this would yield us a percentage-change model.

Special Industry Models

The General Model

The general model outlined in this chapter does not distinguish between various types of industries; it is most relevant for the manufacturing industries oriented to the national market. Some industries, such as mining, cannot be subjected to the same analysis as the manufacturing industries; we have therefore devised special models for nonmanufacturing industries that require special treatment.

We divided the industry sector employment data into three major classifications: industries principally serving a national market, industries dependent upon the intermediate demands of local economic activity, and industries directly dependent upon local final demand (personal consumption). National industries can be further split into resource-based and nonresource-based categories. Industries which sell to national or at least multicounty markets are distinct from those which sell only locally. The response of a nationally oriented industry such as textile manufacturing to a change in conditions within a county is different from the response of a local industry such as retail trade. Local change has little effect on the market for textiles but does affect the desirability of the county as a place to locate. On the other hand, for an industry such as retail trade, local changes affect both the producing site and the market. Local-market industries are of two types: those which offer business services to other industries, such as trucking, and those which are more population oriented, such as retail trade.

For several reasons, we have disaggregated the data for nationally oriented and business-service industries as much as possible, leaving minimal detail in the population-oriented industries. The national industries are important for regional development, as they provide income-earning exports and enable the community to support an infrastructure of business-service and population-oriented industries. In addition, the national and business-service industries require closer analysis than the population-oriented sectors; presumably their location requirements vary more from sector to sector than do the requirements of businesses dependent primarily upon local population and purchasing power. Finally, the national employment projections of Almon, with which we benchmark our forecasts, are considerably more detailed in the producing sectors than in the population-oriented sectors.

As described in Chapter 5, we used employment data supplied by the Office of Business Economics. Observations by county are available for 1940, 1950, and 1960.[4] The data list of 32 industries, is shown in column 2 of Table 3–1. In column 1 are the 24 combinations of the OBE industries distinguished for this study. The third column specifies each industry as national (N), business service (S), population-oriented (P), or some combination of the three. The letters "RB" identify a resource-based industry. Many industries fall into more than one category. Not only do some firms serve both businesses and final consumers, but some of our industrial categories aggregate over firms belonging to different categories. Our industry 21 (business services, etc.), for instance, contains both advertising, sold almost exclusively to business, and automobile repair service and garages, which deal primarily with individuals.

Industries 1 through 3 and 5 through 14 all sell to a national market, with two partial exceptions. The food and kindred products (5) and the printing and publishing (9) industries both have a strong local orientation. Much food processing takes place near the market rather than where the food is produced; a large portion of the printing and publishing business is output of local journals.

Industry 4, construction, and industries 15 through 19, transportation and utilities, serve both business and the local populace. These sectors have a "national" content as well. For example, utility installations in a community may serve large regions of the United States. Airport employees sell to the nation by providing services to flights enroute. As these industries are disaggregated to the maximum degree the data will permit, the distinction makes little difference from the point of view of our allocation analysis.

Industry 20 includes industries defined to be purely population oriented. Conceptually, many banking, finance, and insurance activities are national in scope, but industry employment is highly correlated with population. Most observations evidently are for bank offices, small loan offices, and local insurance and real estate agents. The services offered by these sectors tend to be used universally by businesses, so even their business-service functions tie banking, insurance, and real estate to population size.

---

[4]The 1940 data were not used. Much of the 1940 socioeconomic data are not comparable to the 1950 and 1960 data.

Table 3–1

Comparison of CRA and OBE Industry Classifications

24 CRA Industries	32 OBE Industries	Type of Industry*
1. Agriculture	Same as CRA	N,RB
2. Forestry and fisheries	"	N,RB
3. Mining	"	N,RB
4. Contract construction	"	SP
5. Food and kindred products	"	NP
6. Textiles	"	NP
7. Apparel	"	NP
8. Lumber, wood, and furniture	"	NP
9. Printing and publishing	"	NP
10. Chemical and allied products	"	NP
11. Machinery	"	NP
12. Motor vehicles and equipment	"	NP
13. Other transportation equipment	"	NP
14. Miscellaneous manufacturing	"	NP
15. Railroads	"	SP
16. Trucking and warehousing	"	SP
17. Other transportation	"	SP
18. Communications	"	SP
19. Utilities	"	SP
20. Consumer services	20. Wholesale trade	P
21. Business and professional services	21. Food and dairy products stores	P
22. Public administration	22. Eating and drinking places	P
23. Armed Forces	23. Miscellaneous retail	P
24. Industry not reported	24. Banking, finance, and insurance	SP
	25. Hotels and personal services	P
	26. Private households	P
	27. Business services	SP
	28. Recreation	P
	29. Medical, education, welfare, and professional	SP
	30. Public	
	31. Armed Forces	
	32. Industry not reported	NSP

* See text.

In many respects, industry 21 activities are much like those in industry 20. But many activities in industry 21, particularly advertising; miscellaneous business services; medical services; some of the educational services; and legal, engineering, and miscellaneous professional services, require a higher degree of professionalism than most of the population-oriented industries. The industry 21 group is supported by a different type of community and requires different personnel than the industry 20 group. This distinction may be ephemeral in practice, but it appears worth investigating.

The public sector would be almost wholly population and business service oriented, were it not for the presence of federal public administration employees in the data. These employees "sell" to the nation and tend to be concentrated in large federal administration centers. Unlike the case of postal service and state and local public administration, federal public administration employment is not highly correlated with population.

We have made no attempt to allocate projected employment for the Armed Forces (industry 23) or for "industry not reported" (industry 24). We have no faith in our ability to develop a rational explanation for the physical distribution of Department of Defense installations. Implicitly, the "industry not reported" category has been allocated across the other industries in proportion to their projected employments.

The model described above was applied directly to most of the industries in Table 3–1, but special treatment was required for the resource-based industries and for the transportation industries. The form of this special treatment is described below.

Resource-Based Industries

Our aim has been to explain changes in industrial activity in an area by the presence or absence of certain socioeconomic factors. For some industries, however, location decisions rest strictly upon the presence or absence of natural resources. Activity will depend upon the local supply of resources and the national demand for the resource.

The resource-based industry categories distinguished in our study are agriculture, mining, and forestry and fisheries. Again, employment is used as a measure of industrial activity. For the nation as a whole, there has been a general decline of employment in resource-based industries. As not all counties have been equally affected by the broad national trend, we must do more than attribute broad national trends to the county data.

An area's comparative advantage in supporting a resource-based activity depends upon its ability to supply the resource at a low cost relative to other suppliers. For example, the South's relative advantage as a producer of cotton continued until technological innovation made the large, level lands of the Southwest more productive. Similarly, high transportation costs may prevent an area from being a supply source even if it possesses the necessary resources. Thus, transportation innovations can create new areas of low-cost supply, or an area's composition of resources may change.

One useful method used to explain variation in employment by county in industries such as mining or agriculture is to disaggregate these industries as much as possible. For example, the decline of the coal industry relative to the petroleum industry might account for the fact that mining employment has been increasing more rapidly in Arizona than in Pennsylvania. Disaggregation can also account for differences within a sector of changes in labor productivity: e.g., some types of farming have experienced a greater increase in labor productivity than others, thus effecting relative changes in the demand for employment. A complete analysis would require knowledge of the inventory of resource reserves; a decline in production may be the result of depletion of natural resources. However, detailed information of this sort was not available.

At any rate, socioeconomic variables are not sufficient to explain shifts in resource-based industries. The procedure used for analyzing the resource-based industries is described below.

Agriculture. We were able to obtain an indirect breakdown of employment by county for nine crops and were thus able to analyze agriculture in greater detail than does Almon, who presents projections only for "all crops" and "all livestock."

Our procedure was to make a "trial" projection of employment on the basis of the composition of county employment by crop and regional production and productivity indexes for each crop. This preliminary projection assumes that changes in output and productivity by region are invariant with respect to county. We then used the preliminary projection as an independent variable in a regression equation similar to that of the basic model described earlier.

The following data were available for the analysis:

Symbol	Description	Source
E_5^i	Employment in agriculture in county i in 1950	*Census of Population*
E_6^i	Employment in agriculture in county i in 1960	*Census of Population*
R_{A6}	Percent of farmers growing crop A in 1959	*Census of Agriculture*
I_{Aj5}	Index of production of crop A in region j in 1950	Supplement I to *Changes in Farm Production and Efficiency,* 1967 (CFPE)
I_{Aj6}	Index of production of crop A in region j in 1960	
M_{Aj5}	Index of farm production per man hour in crop A in region j in 1950	Supplement IV to *Changes in Farm Production and Efficiency,* 1967 (CFPE)
M_{Aj6}	Index of farm production per man hour in crop A in region j in 1960	

Data were available for the following crops:

CRA Definition	Definition on CFPE Basis
Cash grains	Food grains
Tobacco	Tobacco
Cotton	Cotton
Other field crops	Hay and forage
Vegetables	Vegetables
Fruits and nuts	Fruits and nuts
Poultry	Poultry
Dairy	Milk cows
Other livestock	Meat animals
General	All farm output
Miscellaneous	All farm output

The farm production regions used in the CFPE reports are as follows:

Region	States Included
Northeast	Maine, New Hampshire, Vermont, Massachusetts, Rhode Island, Connecticut, New York, New Jersey, Pennsylvania, Delaware, and Maryland
Lake States	Michigan, Wisconsin, and Minnesota
Corn Belt	Ohio, Indiana, Illinois, Iowa, and Missouri
Northern plains	North Dakota, South Dakota, Nebraska, and Kansas
Appalachia	Virginia, West Virginia, North Carolina, Kentucky, and Tennessee
Southeast	South Carolina, Georgia, Florida, and Alabama
Delta States	Mississippi, Arkansas, and Louisiana
Southern plains	Oklahoma and Texas
Mountain	Montana, Idaho, Wyoming, Colorado, New Mexico, Arizona, Utah, and Nevada
Pacific	Washington, Oregon, and California

A five-step procedure was used to project agricultural employment by county:

1. The regional indexes of the CFPE (I_{Aj6}, I_{Aj5}, M_{Aj6}, M_{Aj5}) were first converted to corresponding county indexes (I_{Ai6}, I_{Ai5}, M_{Ai6}, M_{Ai5}). We thus implicitly assumed that production and productivity trends were the same for all counties in a given region.

2. Using the county indexes calculated in step 1, the estimated 1960 employment $\hat{E}_6^i$ was calculated from 1950 employment under the assumption that changes in output and labor productivity are invariant with respect to county. That is,

$$\hat{E}_6^i = \sum_A (E_5^i \cdot R_{A6}) \frac{I_{Ai6}}{I_{Ai5}} \cdot \frac{M_{Ai5}}{M_{Ai6}} \qquad (3.11)$$

In equation (3.11), total employment in county i is multiplied by R_{A6}, the percent of farmers growing crop A in 1959, to obtain an estimate of employment in crop A in 1950:

$$E_5^i \cdot R_{A6}$$

This figure is then multiplied by the ratio of the index of production of crop A for 1960 to the index of production of crop A for 1950 to obtain an estimate of employment in crop A in 1960, assuming that there is no change in composition of employment and no change in productivity:

$$(E_5^i \cdot R_{A6}) \frac{I_{Ai6}}{I_{Ai5}}$$

To adjust for productivity change, this figure is then multiplied by the ratio of the index of farm production per man-hour in crop A in 1950 to the index of farm production per man-hour in 1960:

$$(E_5^i \cdot R_{A6}) \frac{I_{Ai6}}{I_{Ai5}} \cdot \frac{M_{Ai5}}{M_{Ai6}}$$

This estimate is then summed over all crops to obtain $\hat{E}_6^i$.[5]

3. E_6^i was then regressed on the vector of socioeconomic variables $(\bar{Q})$ and $\hat{E}_6^i$.

$$\ln E_6^i = \alpha + \bar{\beta}\bar{Q}_5 + \gamma \ln \hat{E}_6^i \qquad (3.12)$$

4. Using the regressions calculated in step 3, employment in 1970 was projected using the following equations:

$$E_7^i = \alpha + \bar{\beta}\bar{Q}_6 + \gamma\hat{E}_7^i \qquad (3.13)$$

$$\hat{E}_7^i = \sum_A E_6^i \frac{I_{Ai7}}{I_{Ai6}} \cdot \frac{M_{Ai6}}{M_{Ai7}} \cdot R_{A6} \qquad (3.14)$$

Estimates of I_{Ai7} and M_{Ai7} were calculated using data available through

---

[5] Lack of data forced us to assume that the composition of employment by crop was the same in both 1950 and 1959, an assumption contradicted by our procedure of using different indexes of production and productivity for each crop. However, the relative movements of the indexes are not sufficiently different for the results to be very biased.

1966. The productivity indexes (M_{Ai7}) were projected by graphing the historical data and projecting visually. With the exception of the production of fruits and nuts, which in most regions had erratic movements, there were strong trends for all crops.

The production indexes for 1970 were derived by projecting on the basis of regressions of the historical indexes on total personal consumption and on time. The consumption variable was picked because Almon presents a 1970 projection for it and because it is a good proxy for total personal income. The two independent variables are highly collinear, but collinearity does not affect the accuracy of prediction. In the cases with insignificant fits (that is, cases in which the F-statistic was not significant at the 5 percent level of significance) the 1966 value of the index was used as the prediction for 1970. In the cases in which the regression was significant, we still checked the prediction of the equation against the most recent history of the crop. If the prediction seemed out of line with recent history, we again used the 1966 value as the estimate for 1970.

5. The projected county employments from step 4 were scaled so that their sum equalled the Almon projection for agriculture.

Mining. Our procedure was to disaggregate the county mining employment into as many mining categories as possible and then to project mining employment on the assumption that each county will maintain its share of national production in each category of mining.

County employment data are available only for mining as an aggregate. OBE's 118 industry data by state divides mining into four groups: metallic mining, coal, oil and gas, and nonmetallic mining. This, however, still conceals very important differences in growth rates. Almon's model projects growth until 1970 for six categories:

1.	Nonferrous	4.	Nonmetallic
2.	Coal	5.	Ferrous
3.	Oil and gas	6.	Chemical

An estimate of the percentage distribution of mining by type for these six activities by county was available in the *Census of Mineral Industries* for 1958. Volume II (*Area Statistics*) of this census presents data on mining for each state. At the beginning of the state tables there appears a set of maps on which employment by county is represented by means of circles of different sizes. The maps are published for metal mining, coal mining, oil and gas extraction, and nonmetallic minerals mining. Exact figures for each category could not be determined, but since we were only interested in the percentage composition of mining employment by county, the data available from the maps were adequate for our purposes. To make the data comparable with the Almon mining categories, we used Census Table 4 for each state to distribute metal mining to ferrous and nonferrous mining and nonmetallic minerals mining to chemical and other nonmetallic minerals mining. Table 4 of each state report in the *Census of Mineral Industries* presents county data on the distribution of firms by size class by type of mining, but because the size classes are very broad, (e.g., 0–19 employees, 20–99 employees, 100–249 employees, etc.) precise estimates could not be made. Unfortunately, the 1963 *Census of Mineral Industries* did not present comparable data.

Using the estimated 1958 composition of mining employment for each county we then projected total mining by county by applying the distribution data to the 1960 employment data and using the Almon growth projection for each mining category. As in the case of all other industries, the projected employments were then uniformly scaled so that the total predicted mining employment by sector in 1970 equaled the Almon prediction for mining employment by sector.

It must be stressed that national trends are not the only factors explaining slow growth of employment in mining-intensive counties. Thus, such factors as depletion, the emergence of new competitive areas and materials, and changing access to markets are important in determining local county employment.

Forestry and Fisheries. Because natural resources are obviously of overriding importance in forestry and fisheries and because data on past and future employment are very sparse, we assumed that each county will maintain its share of national growth in forestry and fisheries, as projected by Almon.

Transportation Industries. Employment in several of the CRA industries is directly related to economic activity in the other industries. Industries which might be termed dependent industries include contract construction (4), railroads (15), trucking and warehousing (16), other transportation (17), communications (18), utilities (19), and the two population-oriented industries (20 and 21).

The dependent industry equations were generally estimated with the same variables as the national industries, although the size and income variables were expected to be more significant. The major exception to this generalization is that special variables were constructed for the transportation industry models (industries 15 through 17).

Employment by county is provided by the OBE 32-industries classification for the following modes of transportation:

Industry	Content	OBE 118-Industries Code
15	Railroads and railway express service	062
16	Trucking service	063
	Warehousing and storage	064
17	Street railways and bus lines	065
	Taxicab service	066
	Water transportation	067
	Air transportation	068
	Petroleum and gasoline pipeline	069
	Services incidental to transportation	070

We projected employment in each of these categories by means of the following equation:

$$\ln E_{it} = \alpha + \beta \bar{Q}_{i,t-1} + \gamma \ln W_{it}, \qquad i = 15,17 \qquad (3.15)$$

where

$$W_{it} = a_{i1}E_{1t} + \cdots + a_{in}E_{nt}, \qquad i = 15,17 \qquad (3.16)$$

W is a weighted average of projected employment in every other industry, with the weights (a_{ij}) being the use of transportation mode i by industry j in a base year divided by employment in industry j in a base year. The transportation data were obtained from the 1963 *Census of Transportation, Commodity Transportation Survey;* 1960 data were used for employment.

A possible objection to the procedure adopted for the transportation industries is that current employment by industry (E_{1t} through E_{nt}) is in turn a function of lagged Qs and lagged industry employments and that therefore these latter variables should replace the constructed variable W_{it} in equation (3.16). However, too many variables are involved—in theory, in a reduced-form equation every lagged variable and every exogenous variable should appear. If the specification of W_{it} is correct, using W_{it} increases the efficiency of estimation. Furthermore, to the extent that E_{it} is not explained by $E_{i,t-1}$ and the vector of socioeconomic variables, prediction is improved by using W_{it}, which is constructed from actual E_{it}s.

4

Special Problems of the Model

A number of problems had to be solved before the general model and the special industry models outlined above could be estimated. The most important problems were (1) the presence of observations of zero for some of the variables, (2) the excessively aggregated character of some of the industry data (3) the presence of heteroskedasticity in the error terms, (4) the ambiguities involved in using cross-section regressions for projection, and (5) changes over time of the structural relationships.

The "Zero Problem"

Both theoretical and mathematical problems arise when the data vector for the dependent variable (employment in a given industry for every county) contains zeros. As our model uses the logarithmic form of the dependent variable—employment—we must handle the mathematical difficulties that arise when an attempt is made to use the log of zero as an observation in the regression. The same problem arises with lagged employment, an independent variable, which is also used in logarithmic form. Special treatment of the zero observations was therefore required; we could either eliminate counties with zero observations from the regression sample and treat them separately or we could include these counties in the regression sample and adopt some artificial procedure (such as assigning a value of 1 to all counties with zero employment) to avoid including the log of zero.

The theoretical issues arise from the fact that zero is the lowest value that employment may take: negative employment is impossible. These issues arise in linear as well as in logarithmic models.

Suppose that the true structural relationship indicates zero employment in an industry for a certain range of socioeconomic variables. For example, the relationship between employment (E) and education (Q_1) may appear as in Figure 4–1A and may be described by the following equations:

$$E = a + bQ_1 + u_1, \qquad Q_1 \geqslant 4 \qquad (4.1)$$

$$E = 0 + u_2, \qquad Q_1 < 4; \ u_2 \geqslant 0 \qquad (4.2)$$

The level of education has a marginal impact of b on employment. Although the function $E = a + bQ_1$ becomes negative at values of Q_1 less than 4, values of Q_1 less than 4 will not produce negative employment.

37

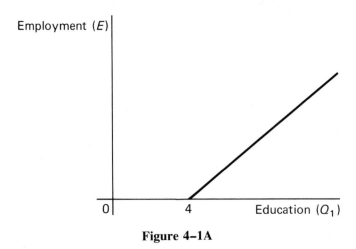

Employment (E)

0   4   Education (Q_1)

Figure 4–1A

Thus, a county with a level of education of 1 is worse off than a county with a level of 3.9, even though both have zero employment, as the latter county does not need a great improvement in its level of education in order to enter the region of positive employment.

As a result of random disturbance, we would expect to observe a scatter of points such as that in Figure 4–1B.

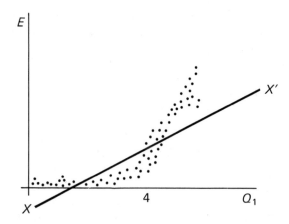

E

X'

4   Q_1

X

Figure 4–1B

Ordinary regression analysis would lead to a predicted relationship similar to XX'. Clearly, the slope of this line will be biased downward. The bias would be present regardless of the random disturbances but it is made worse by the fact that the distribution of the disturbance term is also truncated by the nonnegativity constraint.

The issue is further complicated if the socioeconomic conditions required to generate employment in a given industry are different when there is no past employment in that industry from when there is past employment. It may be easier to expand employment in an industry than it is to establish that industry for the first time in a county. For that matter, entirely different variables and functional forms may be relevant for the establishment of a new industry in a county. Such a hypothesis is similar to that expressed in equation (3.2).

One procedure that might be used to avoid the zeros problem would be to remove the zero observations from the sample. This procedure runs the risk of eliminating counties whose socioeconomic characteristics would generate positive employment but which have no actual employment because of random disturbances and of including counties which should have zero employment but do not because of the disturbance. A common source of disturbance is the fact that the employment data classify workers by place of residence and not by their place of employment.

We have handled the zeros problem by separating the data for a particular industry into four groups: (1) counties with zero employment in both 1950 or 1960; (2) counties with zero employment in 1950 but positive employment in 1960; (3) counties with positive employment in both 1950 and 1960; and (4) counties with positive employment in 1950 but zero employment in 1960.

Before applying the basic model described in the previous chapter, we had to correct for the existence of zeros. On the basis of 1950 and 1960 data we wished to predict which counties would pass from no employment in 1960 to a positive level of employment in 1970 and which counties would pass from positive employment in 1960 to no employment in 1970. We therefore wished to discriminate between counties in categories (1) and (2) on the one hand, and between counties in categories (3) and (4) on the other. In the first case, we wished to identify the socioeconomic factors associated with counties which passed from zero employment in 1950 to positive employment in 1960; and in the second case, to distinguish the socioeconomic factors associated with counties which passed from a positive to a zero rate of employment. For prediction purposes, we then assumed that the relationships found to be relevant for 1950 and 1960 are relevant for 1960 and 1970.

We chose discriminant analysis to distinguish the relevant categories. Discriminant analysis isolates the linear combination of variables which best distinguishes the elements in one set (e.g., those counties with positive employment) from the elements in another set (e.g., those counties with zero employment). To do this, a value of 1 is assigned to all counties in the first set and a value of 0 to all counties in the second set, and a regression is then calculated using the vector of ones and zeros as the dependent variable and the set of socioeconomic variables as the independent variables. The calculated equation then provides a linear combination of the socioeconomic variables by which the counties may be ranked.

Two discriminant analyses (D_1 and D_2) were performed for each industry. In the first (D_1) we discriminated between counties in categories (1) and (2) and in the second (D_2) we discriminated between counties in categories (3) and (4).

		EMPLOYMENT		
		1950	*1960*	*Regression*
D_1: Discriminant set 1	Case 1	0	0	
	Case 2	0	>0	R_1
D_2: Discriminant set 2	Case 3	>0	0	
	Case 4	>0	>0	R_2

The forms of the discriminant equations were the same as the form of the model presented earlier, except that lagged employment obviously could not be included as a variable in the first set of discriminant analyses. For those counties in the two sets for which positive employment was predicted, we then calculated regressions (R_1 and R_2) to predict the magnitude of employment. The R_2 equations were identical in form to equation (3.10). The R_1 equations were identical except that lagged employment could not be included.

The purpose of the two discriminant functions was to isolate those counties expected to have zero employment in a given industry for 1970. An average of 377 counties (out of 3,097) had zero employment in a given industry for 1950. Of these, about 18.3 percent moved to a positive level of employment for 1960. Of the remaining 2,595 counties (average) having 1950 employment in a given industry, only 8 percent moved to zero employment in 1960. For the subset of counties with zero employment in 1950, we estimated a function to predict those counties from among the zero-employment counties in 1960 expected to have nonzero employment for a given industry in 1970. To be selected, we required that a county's discriminant score be significantly greater than zero at a 5 percent one-tail t-test level. In predicting zero cases from among those having positive 1960 employment, we required that the discriminant score be significantly less than 1 at a similar test level.

It should be pointed out that the choice of a 5 percent one-tail t-test value as a discriminant cutoff is rather arbitrary when we consider that in all likelihood the disturbance distributions are not normal. Figure 4–2 depicts a hypothetical structure of discriminant scores distributed about the actual values of 0 and 1. If each segment of the distribution has error terms that are normally distributed with a zero mean, with both having the same variance, then a *t*-test based on the equation standard error of estimate would be equivalent to a *t*-test on one section of the distribution. If this assumption is violated only to the extent that the two parts of the distribution have different variances, then the *t*-test is still appropriate except that the confidence level is incorrect.

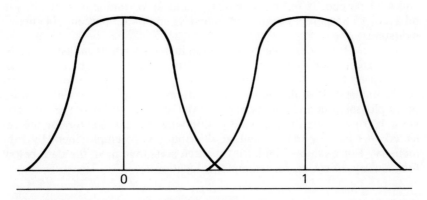

Figure 4–2. Predicted Discriminant Scores for a Well-Separated Function

It is likely, unfortunately, that the above assumptions were violated in a more severe manner. Not only may the error distributions be skewed, but there is no assurance whatsoever that each segment of the distribution has a zero mean disturbance. With these problems in addition to a general lack of separation of the discriminant groups, there were no clear criteria to follow in choosing a score cutoff. The cutoffs chosen above are biased in favor of a county retaining its current status. In the absence of more substantial evidence such a bias is probably warranted.

Aggregation Problems

As the only industry data available by county contain only 32 industry categories, many of the categories are quite heterogeneous in composition. Industry 14, for example, contains such diverse sub-industries as

tobacco manufactures, petroleum refining, blast furnaces, and watches
and clocks. Because the determinants of employment in tobacco manufacture are likely to differ from those in petroleum refining or in blast furnaces, more disaggregated data would have been desirable.

While more disaggregated data are not available by county, they are
available by state. If each state had the same industry composition in
each of the 32 OBE industries, state data would not add any information.
Industry composition does, however, vary by state. For example, if we
divide Industry 14 into tobacco manufactures, light industry, and heavy
industry (primarily oil refineries and metal works) for 1960, we find that
in North Carolina 38.92 percent of industry-14 employment is in tobacco,
45.45 percent is in light industry, and 15.63 percent is in heavy industry;
in Maine 0.11 percent is in tobacco, 95.06 percent is in light industry,
and 4.83 percent is in heavy industry; and in Wyoming, 0 percent is in
tobacco, 15.35 percent is in light industry, and 84.65 percent is in heavy
industry.

To adjust for excess aggregation in industries such as industry 14, we
used intercept and coefficient dummies for selected variables. The procedure used for coefficient dummies is very similar to that used for intercept dummies.[1] Postulating that the marginal impact of certain variables
on employment in an industry varies with the composition of the industry,
we constructed the dummies by multiplying the data vector for the selected variables by the percentage distributions of employment by sub-
industry. For example, suppose for three states we have the data below
for industry 14 (Q_i is, for example, Education).

	Q_i	% in Tobacco	% in Light Industry	% in Heavy Industry
North Carolina	10.2	0.3892	0.4545	0.1563
Maine	12.7	0.0011	0.9506	0.0483
Wyoming	13.6	0	0.1535	0.8465

The three slope dummies for Q_i are then:[2]

	Q_i	D_1	D_2	D_3
North Carolina	10.2	3.97	4.64	1.59
Maine	12.7	0.02	12.07	0.61
Wyoming	13.6	0	2.09	11.51

[1] See J. Johnston, *Econometric Methods* (New York: McGraw-Hill, 1963), pp. 221–228.
[2] As Q_i is a linear combination of D_1, D_2, and D_3, all four variables cannot be entered into the regression at once.

The basic model postulates that the socioeconomic variables have a marginal input on the logarithm of employment which is measured by their slope coefficients in the regressions. The use of ordinary slope and intercept dummies tests the hypothesis that the mere presence of, say, tobacco manufactures alters the functional relationship. The use of slope coefficients which take into account the percentage composition of an industry in each state tests the effect of a percentage increase in, say, employment in tobacco manufactures, rather than the effect of the mere presence or absence of tobacco manufacturing.

Methods of Projection

For each industry, four basic equations were estimated:

1. A discriminant function choosing counties having positive 1960 employment from the subset of counties having zero employment in 1950.
2. A discriminant function choosing counties continuing to have positive 1960 employment from the subset of counties having positive 1950 employment.
3. A regression predicting the level of 1960 employment for those counties actually moving from zero 1950 employment to positive 1960 employment.
4. A regression predicting the level of 1960 employment for those counties having employment in both 1950 and 1960.

Certain conceptual problems arise when these four equations are adapted to predict those counties which will have zero employment in 1970 and the rate of employment for all other counties in 1970. These problems involve (1) how to interpret the regression coefficients in all four equations and (2) what acceptance and rejection criteria to use in the discriminant functions.

The Cross-Section Problem

Certain special problems arise because we are using cross-section regressions to make projections over time. In particular, a problem arises in interpreting the $\beta_j Q_j$s. For example, in the cross-sectional equations the following two interpretations of the median income coefficient are not distinguishable: (1) Employment differs according to differences in median income *relative* to the national average, and (2) employment varies with the absolute changes in median income. Within a single cross-section only relative differences can be distinguished. In projecting 1970 employment, however, the two interpretations yield different results.

If we were to accept the first interpretation, the median income coefficient would be scaled down by the ratio of the 1960 to the 1970 national median incomes. If each coefficient were interpreted in this manner, the values of the 1970 coefficients would change relative to each other compared to 1960. If the second interpretation were accepted, the absolute coefficient values would be retained, but such a decision would increase the *relative* importance of variables with a positive trend such as income or education compared to variables with mean levels which are invariant over time.

There is a third interpretation which allows the absolute values of Q variables to be significant, but which has the same operational significance as interpretation (1) above. Suppose that the absolute value, say, Q_A, is relevant, where

$$Q_A = Q_N Q_R \tag{4.3}$$

$$Q_N = \text{national } Q \text{ level} \tag{4.4}$$

$$Q_R = \text{local relative } Q \text{ level} \tag{4.5}$$

If we specify that in our logarithmic function $\ln E_{60}$ is linearly related to Q_N and Q_R, we have the following:

$$\ln E_{60} = \ln c + \mu \ln E_{50} + \bar{\beta}_N \bar{Q}_N + \bar{\beta}_R \bar{Q}_R \tag{4.6}$$

$$E_{60} = c E_{50}^\mu \exp(\bar{\beta}_N \bar{Q}_N + \bar{\beta}_R \bar{Q}_R) \tag{4.7}$$

$$E_{60} = [c \exp(\bar{\beta}_N \bar{Q}_N)] E_{50}^\mu \exp(\bar{\beta}_R \bar{Q}_R) \tag{4.8}$$

$$E_{60} = c^* E_{50}^\mu \exp(\bar{\beta}_R \bar{Q}_R) \tag{4.9}$$

Similarly, if we specify $\ln E_{60}$ to be logarithmically related to Q_A, we obtain the following:

$$\ln E_{60} = \ln c + \mu \ln E_{50} + \beta_A \ln Q_A \tag{4.10}$$

$$= \ln c + \mu \ln E_{50} + \beta_A \ln Q_N + \beta_A \ln Q_R \tag{4.11}$$

$$= (\ln c + \beta_A \ln Q_N) + \mu \ln E_{50} + \beta_A \ln Q_R \tag{4.12}$$

$$= \ln c^* + \mu \ln E_{50} + \beta_A \ln Q_R \tag{4.13}$$

In either case the effect of the absolute level of $\bar{Q}$, as opposed to its relative level, is included in the constant, if an additive relationship is specified in the logarithmic form. As the adjustment of our forecasts to control totals takes the form of altering the constant terms in each equation, absolute effects are included in the adjustment. We can therefore treat the *relative* level of $\bar{Q}$ as the relevant factor, while not ruling out a certain class of absolute Q effects.

Given the acceptance of the above criteria, we must still decide whether to hold relative coefficients constant, or whether to hold relative beta weights constant. If the variance of a given Q_R^i increases from 1950 to 1960, the assumption of a constant coefficient implies that this particular Q_R^i will have a greater impact on the variance of $\ln E_{70}$ than it did on $\ln E_{60}$. Given possible changes in the variance of all Q_R^is, such an interpretation allows for a possible change over time in the relative power of different Q_R^is, as well as a different predicted variance for $\ln E_{70}$ than was the case for $\ln E_{60}$.

If we hold relative beta weights constant, on the other hand, we restrict each variable to have a fixed influence on the variance of $\ln E_{70}$. While neither assumption is likely to be correct as a polar extreme, the first alternative is less restrictive as an approximation.

We therefore chose to interpret each Q_j as a value relative to the national average, and β_j to be scaled such that

$$\sum_{i=1}^{n} \beta_j Q_j^i$$

is invariant from 1950 to 1960 for each Q_j, where $i = 1, ..., n$ refers to the 3,097 counties in the model. Any discrepancies with the control totals were thus corrected by making an appropriate uniform adjustment in the logarithmic constant.[3]

Problems Unique to the Discriminant Functions

Two adjustments were made to the estimated equations: first, the coefficient adjustment just described, and second, a consistency adjustment in the constant term to coordinate the results with the Almon control totals. This second adjustment also absorbs any absolute effects which were omitted from the model specification. For the discriminant functions, however, we did not have this second adjustment as a safeguard. If the Q_js are important only in their relative effects, there is no way in

---

[3] As $\ln E_{50}$ is a scale variable, it seems reasonable to assume that its coefficient should retain its absolute value. Relative adjustments were therefore made only in the Q variables.

46

which absolute effects can have an impact without seriously distorting the discriminant functions. While we expect that a relative value assumption is reasonable, it is on less secure ground for the discriminant functions than for the regressions.

In treating lagged employment (or some other scale variable) in an absolute manner, we are implicitly assuming that if all counties increase in absolute size (population or employment), the appearance of a zero observation for a given industry classification is less likely. This assumption is probably more reasonable than the alternative assumption that a county of a given *relative* size has a given likelihood of yielding a zero observation regardless of its absolute size.

**Problems Involving Changes in the
Relationships Over Time**

The assumption that future time periods are governed by the same structural relationships which have been estimated from historical data creates a well-known problem in statistical estimation. Two aspects of this general problem are especially worthy of note.

First, we have specified that employment in 1960 is a function of 1950 variables. Our implicit assumption is that the speed of response to lagged variables will remain the same in the 1960–1970 period as it was in 1950–1960. A specialized violation of this assumption would arise if the speed of response to each lagged variable increased by a uniform rate. If this were to happen, we would not obtain a prediction of the 1970 employment distribution, but rather a prediction for some earlier year. A more likely violation of the assumption would be that the speeds of response to lagged variables have changed in a diverse manner.

Second, the predicted range of discriminant scores for 1970 might be substantially different from the 0–1 range of 1960. A number of explanations might be advanced for such a result, each of which must be kept in mind in interpreting the results. For example, the basic structural relationships may have changed, in which case the discriminant scores become meaningless unless we can determine the nature of the structural changes. Alternatively, our treatment of relative and absolute socioeconomic effects may have been incorrect, resulting in incorrectly scaled discriminant scores, or finally, the discriminant structure may have remained the same, with differences in the score distributions reflecting legitimate changes in the likelihood of zero and nonzero observations.

Despite the above pitfalls, in the absence of contrary evidence we interpreted the discriminant functions literally, with the same adjustments in relative Q values as in the case for regressions. Decisions on the discriminant functions were made independently of adjustments to the Almon projections.

Problems Arising from Heteroskedasticity
of the Disturbance Terms

There is reason to believe that the two regression sets may have hetero-skedastic disturbance terms. Specifically, there is probably a systematic relationship between the size of the variance and the population (or employment) size of the county. Fortunately, the possible presence of heteroskedasticity affects only the efficiency of the estimates, not their consistency.

The choice of a logarithmic estimating equation should roughly correct for heteroskedasticity, in that the smaller observations have a heavier weight. In relative terms, the upper ranges of the disturbances are scaled down and the lower ranges are scaled up. However, if a small county is more likely to have a given error disturbance than a large county, the logarithmic form would overcorrect for heteroskedasticity. In any event, we have attempted no formal adjustment for heteroskedasticity.

5 Implementation of the Model

The implementation of the model developed in the earlier chapters involved massive data processing problems. The model required extensive collection and processing of data for each of the 3,097 counties in the United States. In this chapter we describe the selection of the data and the empirical procedures adopted in implementing the model.

Data Used in the Analysis

It must be stressed that our objective in selecting data was to provide a 1970 projection of county employment by industry. The necessity of providing county estimates required that both the industrial employment measures and the social and economic explanatory variables be available in machine-processable form and be compatible over the time span being examined.

Industry Employment Measures

The county industrial employment data were taken from the 1950 and 1960 censuses of population published in *Growth Patterns in Employment by County 1940–1960* by the Office of Business Economics (OBE), U.S. Department of Commerce. These data are disaggregated into 32 industry categories.

As the industry employment data are drawn from the Censuses of Population, the data are collected by place of *residence,* and are therefore not necessarily equivalent to data collected by place of *employment.* This can be a particularly acute problem at the fringes of large metropolitan areas and in counties where a major population center lies near the county border, making a large disparity likely between the actual level and mix of industrial activity in a county and the mix of industries in which the county's residents are employed.

Unfortunately, the 32 industry categories in the OBE data contain significantly more defining detail for service industries than for primary and manufacturing industries. For example, a single category, other and miscellaneous manufacturing, includes such diverse industries as tobacco manufacturing, watches and clock manufacturing, and blast furnaces.

Another difficulty with the OBE categories is that a particular industry in one area of the country may have a composition quite different from that of the same industry in another area. For example, forestry and fisheries employment is likely to be mainly forestry employment in Idaho and mainly fisheries employment in New Jersey. Industry 14, miscellaneous manufacturing, may include predominately tobacco manufacturing in North Carolina and predominately leather products in Massachusetts.

To approach the problem of industry definition, we obtained from OBE further breakdowns of the census data on the state level to 118 industries for 1950 and 1960. Appendix C presents a list of the 118 industries, arranged according to correspondence with the more aggregated 32-industry group. As described in Chapter 4, we used this finer breakdown in certain instances in which we felt that a given classification was too broad for our purpose.

A final problem was the heterogeneous nature of the county unit. Existing county boundaries are not generally a reflection of any uniform criterion, but rather result from historical political circumstance and, in some cases, geographic conditions. Vast differences in land area, population, and other factors occur among states and even within a state. For example, Georgia has 157 counties while Arizona, with nearly double the land area, has only 14. Alpine County, California, had 397 people in 1960; Los Angeles County had over 6 million. While these examples may not be typical, they serve to illustrate the lack of uniformity in county characteristics and can be extended to almost any descriptive variables reported.

As described in Chapter 3, we compressed the OBE 32-industry list into a 22-industry list by aggregating service-oriented industries into two groups: industries 20 through 26 and industry 28 composed the first group (CRA industry 20), while industries 27 and 29 comprised the second (CRA industry 21). Table 3–1 presents the correspondence between the OBE industry classification and the CRA industry classification used in this study. For the 24 CRA industries, no econometric relationships were estimated for mining, forestry and fisheries, the Armed Forces, or industry not reported. In addition, as described in Chapter 3, equations for agriculture and the transportation industries were estimated by special ad hoc procedures.

Explanatory Variables

The variables used to explain the changes in employment by industry were also required on a county basis in machine-processable form. The basic sources were the *County and City Data Books* for 1962 and 1952, published by the Bureau of the Census, containing primarily 1960 and 1950 data, respectively.

Other data available in the required form for analysis included data on

(1) the availability of transportation facilities, by air, water, rail, and highway; (2) climate, soil, and terrain; (3) the distance to nearest metropolitan areas of various sizes; (4) agricultural activity; (5) mining activity; (6) the cost of oil, gas, and electricity at the state level.

The form of our model required us to predict 1960 employment as a function of 1950 employment and 1950 socioeconomic variables stated in such a way that they are scale-free (i.e., proportion, averages, etc.). The following selection criteria were used:

1. Variables that represented a linear combination of other included variables were eliminated as redundant (with the exception of the dummy variables).
2. Because the models were ultimately to be used with 1960 data to predict 1970 values, variables were not used for which comparable values were not available for both 1950 and 1960.
3. When there existed a group of variables that could be expected to measure the same factor, the group was reduced to one or two chosen on the basis of a priori examination.

The socioeconomic variables chosen for inclusion in the preliminary analysis are described in Table 5–1. Two variables, the logarithm of population aged 21–64 (a labor force availability proxy), and total employment, were retained for use as scaling variables, as described in Chapter 3.

Model Estimation Procedures

Several issues were involved in determining the exact form of the equations. First, the regression and discriminant functions for those counties having no employment in a given industry for 1950 did not have a "scale variable," such as lagged industry employment. For these cases, lagged total employment and total population aged 21–64 were tested in logarithmic form as scale substitutes.

Second, we found that in many cases a general scale variable such as the two mentioned above retained its significance in the presence of lagged industry employment. We therefore allowed for the possibility of including such a scale variable in the equations.

Third, by accepting the OBE 32-industry classification, in effect we assumed that all industries in a given grouping react in a homogenous manner to socioeconomic characteristics. In fact, as we have seen earlier the composition of a given industry can be quite different in different states.

As described in Chapter 4, slope and coefficient dummies were used

Table 5–1

Explanatory Variables

Variable Number	Variable Name
1–22	Logarithm of employment in 1950 of corresponding industry sector.
23–44	Logarithm of employment in 1960 of corresponding industry sector.
45–110	Dummy variables indicating 0 employment in 1950 or 1960 for all industries.
111	Logarithm of special constructed variable for agriculture (sector 4):

$$\ln E_6^i = \sum_A (E_5^i \cdot R_{A_6}) \frac{I_{A i_6}}{I_{A i_5}} \cdot \frac{M_{A i_5}}{M_{A i_6}}$$

(See Chapter 3.)

| 112 | Logarithm of special constructed variable for railroads (sector 15): |

$$W_{15} = a_{15,1} E_{1,t} + \cdots + a_{15,n} E_{n,t}$$

(See Chapter 3.)

| 113 | Special constructed variable for trucks (sector 16): |

$$W_{16} = a_{16,1} E_{1,t} + \cdots + a_{16,n} E_{n,t}$$

(See Chapter 3.)

| 114 | Special constructed variable for other transportation (sector 17): |

$$W_{17} = a_{17,1} E_{1,t} + \cdots + a_{17,n} E_{n,t}$$

(See Chapter 3.)

115	$\dfrac{\text{Population, 1950}}{\text{Population, 1940}}$.
116	Proportion of population nonwhite.
117	Population density $\left(\dfrac{\text{population}}{\text{area}}\right)$.
118	Proportion of population urban.
119	Proportion of population rural farm.
120	Proportion of population aged 21–64 years.
121	Logarithm of population aged 21–64 years.
122	Live births (one year) per family.
123	Proportion of persons 25 years and over with less than 5 years education.
124	Proportion of persons 25 years and over with less than 12 years education.
125	Proportion of labor force male $\left(\dfrac{\text{males in labor force}}{\text{total labor force}}\right)$.
126	Proportion of labor force unemployed.
127	Proportion of total employed persons employed in mining.
128	Proportion of total employed persons employed in manufacturing.
129	Proportion of total employed persons employed in wholesale–retail trade.

Table 5–1 (continued)

Variable Number	Variable Name
130	Average family size $\left(\dfrac{\text{population}}{\text{number of families}}\right)$.
131	Median family income.
133	Proportion of dwelling units built after 1940.
134	$\dfrac{\text{Time and savings deposits}}{\text{population}}$
135	Normal maximum temperature, annual (from data compiled from U.S. Weather Bureau records by Charles River Associates).
136	Normal precipitation, annual (from Weather Bureau data, see variable 135).
137	Distance to nearest SMSA of over 250,000 population center, from census data processed by Charles River Associates.
138	Distance to nearest SMSA of over 1,000,000 population (from census population centers data, see variable 137).
139	Terrain variability index (derived by Charles River Associates from mapping contour interval data supplied by Geological Survey, U.S. Department of the Interior).
140	Relative extent of unionization in state, 1953 (from *Changes in the Location of Manufacturing in the United States Since 1929*, by Victor R. Fuchs).
141	Railroad line variable (number of railroad lines running through a county, derived from map data).*
142	Highways variable (number of major highways serving the largest population center in each county, value limited to nine for large cities, derived from map data).*
143	Cost of oil in state (in dollars per barrel, from 1958 *Census of Manufactures*).
144	Cost of gas in state (in dollars per thousand cubic feet, from 1958 *Census of Manufactures*).
145	Cost of electricity in state (in dollars per 1,000 kilowatt hours, from 1958 *Census of Manufactures*).
146	Water availability variable (variable to indicate existence of seacoast or navigable waterway in county, having a value of one if it exists and zero otherwise, derived from maps and Corps of Engineers data).
147	Median age of population.
148	Land area.
149	Logarithm of total employment.
150	$\dfrac{\text{Employment in manufacturing}}{\text{Number of establishments}}$.
151	State proportion of food and kindred products (CRA industry 5) engaged in dairy products (OBE industry 10).†
152	State proportion of food and kindred products (CRA industry 5) engaged in canning (OBE industry 11).
153	State proportion of lumber and wood products employment (CRA industry 8) engaged in furniture manufactures (OBE industry 27).

(*continued*)

Table 5–1 (continued)

Variable Number	Variable Name
154	State proportion of machinery and equipment manufactures employment (CRA industry 11) engaged in the manufacture of office and electrical machinery (OBE industries 33 and 35).
155	State proportion of transport equipment employment (CRA industry 13) engaged in the manufacture of aircraft (OBE industry 37).
156	State proportion of transport equipment employment (CRA industry 15) engaged in the manufacture of ships (OBE industry 38).
157	State proportion of miscellaneous manufactures (CRA industry 14) employment engaged in the manufacture of tobacco products (OBE industry 40).
158	State proportion of miscellaneous manufactures (CRA industry 14) engaged in the manufacture of petroleum and petroleum products (OBE industries 44 and 45).
159	State proportion of miscellaneous manufactures (CRA industry 14) engaged in the manufacture of products of blast furnaces, and other metal industries (OBE industries 56 and 57).
160	Variable 158 plus variable 159.
161	Variable 151 times variable 137.
162	Variable 152 times variable 137.
163	Variable 153 times variable 123.
164	Variable 154 times variable 123.
165	Variable 155 times variable 123.
166	Variable 156 times variable 140.
167	Variable 157 times variable 123.
168	Variable 160 times variable 123.

SOURCE: U.S. Department of Commerce, Bureau of the Census, *County and City Data Books, 1952* and *1962* (Washington, D.C.: Government Printing Office, 1952 and 1962), unless otherwise noted.

*It was not possible without prohibitive expense to calculate the total mileage of railway lines or highways in each county.

†OBE industry numbers are from the OBE 118-industry list.

for particularly heterogenous industries to test the hypothesis that the functional relationships between county employment in a given industry and county socioeconomic characteristics change as the state composition of the industry changes.

The following intercept-affecting dummies were tested in the relevant industry equations:

1. State proportion of food and kindred products employment engaged in dairy products and in canning, respectively.
2. State proportion of lumber, wood, and furniture products employment engaged in furniture manufactures.

3. State proportion of machinery employment engaged in the manufacture of office and electrical machinery.
4. State proportion of other transportation equipment employment engaged in the manufacture of aircraft and in the manufacture of ships.
5. State proportion of miscellaneous manufacturing employment engaged in the manufacture of tobacco products, petroleum and petroleum products, and blast furnaces and other metal industries, respectively.

By including these state proportions in an equation, we were in effect allowing the intercept to vary with changes in the state proportions, while holding all the socioeconomic coefficients constant. Such a procedure is not satisfactory, however, if two or more industries within a group react differently to a given socioeconomic characteristic. As described in Chapter 4, this problem was approached with the use of coefficient dummies. To reduce the number of regressions to manageable proportions, we limited our testing to one socioeconomic characteristic for each of the cases in which we had used intercept dummies, as described earlier. In most cases we assumed that the most crucial difference among industries would be skill requirements. As we found that the proportion of the adult population having less than five years of education served as a useful proxy for the skill level of the local labor force, we generally tested for homogeneity of that coefficient. Food products, for which we used distance to nearest SMSA with a population of at least 250,000, and shipbuilding, for which we used a water availability dummy, were exceptions to this general variable choice.

Fourth, the sheer magnitude of the data processing required some simplification of the statistical procedure. Given 63 equations to estimate across different subsets of the 3,097 counties in the contiguous United States, we were required to calculate separate correlation matrices for each combination of sample points which was used. With 35 socioeconomic variables in addition to all employment variables, discriminant dummies, and intercept and slope dummies, it was inefficient to include all socioeconomic variables for testing purposes in each correlation matrix. For this reason, we chose subsets of socioeconomic variables for each equation on the basis of a 531 county sample, which was stratified to give each region of the country a representation proportional to its population. A variable was retained for a given equation only if its inclusion reduced the standard error of estimate across the sample counties. In the cases in which the 531 county sample did not provide a sufficient subset of observations for a given equation, we used the same variable selection which was found to be significant for other regressions within the given industry grouping.

After individual equation matrices had been reduced in size by the above procedure, we then estimated the equations of our model using data for all 3,097 counties. Variables which failed to reduce the standard error of estimate for a given equation were omitted in this final stage.

6

Presentation and Interpretation of the Estimated Equations and Forecasts

Introduction

Before we present our results, we feel that it is important to summarize the shortcomings of our model, most of which have been discussed earlier. The reader should be well aware of these limitations in order to avoid improper use of the results. It should be pointed out, furthermore, that the limitations encountered in our model are common to any regional analysis; every effort has been made to reduce these shortcomings to a minimum.

The largest biases probably arise from a number of unavoidable specification errors, although it is possible that some of the errors are offsetting:

1. The specification of functional forms had to be based on a priori knowledge. While our formulations may have intuitive appeal, it is quite possible that other functional forms may be more representative of the true structure. Furthermore, it is possible that different functional forms are relevant for different industries, or even that locational decisions in some industries are so random that attempting to formulate a functional relationship with the available socioeconomic variables is a meaningless exercise.

2. Somewhat related to this point, the observed data represent a simultaneous interaction of forces. Our specified model is in fact recursive, but we have probably ignored many simultaneous interactions; furthermore, autocorrelation of the error terms leads to bias. Predictions based on these equations are valid, but the individual slope coefficients may be incorrect. We only know that after all simultaneous interactions have worked themselves out that, for example, a high level of education in a county has been associated in the past with high employment in a given industry.

3. Another unavoidable specification error is that data for all relevant variables are not available, such as, for example, data on social overhead capital.

4. Furthermore, there is no guarantee that the lag response (10 years) specified in the model is representative of the true structure, or that the lag will remain the same for all variables during the projection period. This point is related to the whole general problem of whether the future will be like the present—a problem, of course, for which there can be no solution. However, for reasons of data availability, we were unable to test alternative lag responses.

5. Still in the realm of specification error, there is no guarantee that the particular area and industry units selected (counties and the 22 industry sectors) are at the proper aggregation level. We were forced to use the data in the form in which they were available. Given unlimited computer time, however, it would have been instructive to have performed separate regressions for counties cross-classified by, say, region of the country, total employment, and percentage of rural population. The functional relationships are quite possibly different in each case.

A second general class of problems arose in attempting to make projections on the basis of cross-section equations. First there is a range of possible assumptions for scaling the regression equations; each of these changes the relative allocation of employment among counties. In addition, the interpretation of the discriminant analyses is ambiguous, both with respect to scaling and with respect to selecting the cutoff criteria. While these problems are thoroughly discussed above, the decisions made had to be based on intuitive appeal rather than empirical knowledge, as empirical tests of the various assumptions were impossible with the available data.

Finally, a number of statistical problems were encountered in the empirical analysis. The greatest damage may have been caused by the possible presence of heteroskedasticity, but other assumptions of the theory of ordinary least squares may also have been violated. We did not attempt to correct for bias or inefficiency arising from these difficulties. As the standard statistical procedures in regression analysis have been shown to be robust (that is, their properties are not dependent on the more debatable assumptions of the model),[1] we felt that the benefits to be gained in our case for corrections for such statistical problems as heteroskedasticity were small relative to the large costs involved in making such corrections.

Finally, while analyzing our results, the reader should remember that our criterion for inclusion of variables in the equations was solely whether the inclusion of a variable significantly reduced the standard error of estimate. The reason for adopting this procedure was that the purpose of our equations was primarily that of prediction, and for prediction one need only worry about measuring the correlations of the independent variables with the dependent variables.

Such a procedure, however, leads to difficulties if one tries to infer the true structural relationships from the estimated equations. For example, many of the variables retained had coefficients whose signs were contrary to expectations. As all retained coefficients were statistically significant, the explanation for incorrect signs is probably that the variables in question are proxies for other variables not included as a result of lack of

[1] E. Malinvaud, *Statistical Methods of Econometrics* (Chicago: Rand McNally, 1966), p. 11.

data. While this fact does not affect the accuracy of the model's predictions if the relationships among the variables remain the same in future time periods, it does impair our ability to make inferences about the true structure in general and about causal relationships in particular. For example, the variable "proportion of labor force employed in mining" in the equations in which it appeared was almost invariably negatively correlated with employment in nonmining activities. One cannot, however, jump to the policy conclusion that the mining industry should be discouraged, as the reason for the negative correlation is undoubtedly that mining-intensive counties in general have *other* characteristics which are detrimental to economic activity. Reducing the level of mining employment would probably harm these counties, as such a reduction would probably not have an impact on the socioeconomic characteristics which are the real cause of economic inactivity.

**Results of Discriminant and
Regression Analyses**

As our final model contains 63 equations, and 39 variables appear in at least one equation, a readable presentation of the estimated equations in detail would be impossible. We have therefore attempted to consolidate the results without eliminating important information. The individual equations, however, are presented in Appendix D for the reader who wishes additional information on the final model. We will discuss first the four sets of equations (the two discriminant and the two regression sets); this discussion will be followed by a discussion of the individual variables found to be correlated with employment.

*Discrimination Functions: Cases with Zero
Employment in 1950*

The first set of discriminant functions was designed to separate those counties which had positive 1960 employment in a given industry from those which did not, within the subset of counties which had zero employment in 1950. In the discriminant functions these groups were assigned the values one and zero, respectively. Table 6–1 lists the distribution of these two categories by industry, along with the two remaining subsets of counties which had positive 1950 employment.

For a number of industries there were no counties with zero 1950 employment. On the average, an industry had 277 zero observations, of which an average of 69 (or 24.9 percent) moved to positive 1960 employment. This movement was more than offset by the movement of an average of 225 counties per industry into the zero category for 1960

Table 6–1

Distribution of Counties by Industry, by 1950 and 1960 Employment Status

Industry	Employment Status			
	Zero 1950, Zero 1960	Zero 1950, Not Zero 1960	Not Zero 1950, Zero 1960	Not Zero 1950, Not Zero 1960
1. Agriculture	0	0	2	3,095
2. Forestry and fisheries	530	92	624	1,851
3. Mining	138	75	339	2,545
4. Contract construction	0	0	2	3,095
5. Food and kindred products	54	24	99	2,920
6. Textiles	759	131	721	1,486
7. Apparel	596	224	312	1,965
8. Lumber, wood, and furniture	155	25	253	2,664
9. Printing and publishing	28	8	145	2,916
10. Chemical and allied products	330	124	492	2,151
11. Machinery	122	89	279	2,607
12. Motor vehicles and equipment	862	230	567	1,438
13. Other transportation equipment	795	425	397	1,480
14. Miscellaneous manufacturing	49	29	150	2,869
15. Railroads	57	3	163	2,874
16. Trucking and warehousing	6	1	67	3,023
17. Other transportation	32	20	119	2,926
18. Communications	40	13	174	2,870
19. Utilities	19	10	52	3,016
20. Consumer services	0	0	0	3,097
21. Business and professional services	0	0	0	3,097
22. Public administration	0	0	2	3,095
Total	4,572	1,523	4,959	57,080
Average	208	69	225	2,595

out of a total of 2820 with nonzero observations. This pattern was repeated in almost every industry, with industry 13 (other transportation equipment) being the only industry group in which the zero to nonzero movement exceeded the reverse flow.

Table 6–2 presents the general results of the estimated discriminant

Table 6–2
Results of Discriminant Functions, Zero Employment in 1950

Industry Number	(1) Number of Observations	(2) Mean	(3) Standard Deviation	(4) Number of Right-hand Variables	(5) R^2	(6) F-statistic	(7) Standard Error of Estimate	(8) Discriminant Cutoff[d]	(9) Absolute Sum of Beta Weights × Standard Deviation	(10) Coefficient of Scale Variable
5	78	0.3077	0.4645	2	0.1977	$F_{(2,75)} = 9.24$[a]	0.4216	0.7045	0.2376	0.1074[f]
6	890	0.1472	0.3545	5	0.0774	$F_{(5,884)} = 14.83$[a]	0.3415	0.5635	0.1764	0.0931[g]
7	820	0.2732	0.4459	8	0.2495	$F_{(8,811)} = 33.70$[a]	0.3882	0.6405	0.4532[e]	0.1156[g]
8	180	0.1389	0.3468	2	0.0829	$F_{(2,177)} = 8.00$[a]	0.3340	0.5511	0.1373	0.1020[g]
9	36	0.2222	0.4216	7	0.4634	$F_{(7,28)} = 3.45$[b]	0.3453	0.5874	1.1792[e]	0.1128[g]
10	454	0.2731	0.4461	5	0.1598	$F_{(5,448)} = 17.05$[a]	0.4111	0.6783	0.3811	0.2088[g]
11	211	0.4218	0.4950	3	0.1912	$F_{(3,207)} = 16.32$[a]	0.4484	0.7399	0.3363[e]	0.2293[f]
12	1092	0.2106	0.4079	6	0.1335	$F_{(6,1085)} = 27.87$[a]	0.3808	0.6283	0.2811	0.1208[g]
13	1220	0.3484	0.4766	5	0.1731	$F_{(5,1214)} = 50.84$[a]	0.4343	0.7166	0.2983	0.1332[f]
14	78	0.3718	0.4864	8	0.4273	$F_{(8,69)} = 6.43$[a]	0.3889	0.6495	3.1030[e]	-1.4340,[f] +3.0340[g]
15	60	0.0500	0.2198	4	0.2955	$F_{(4,55)} = 5.77$[a]	0.1911	0.3210	0.2704	-.0665
16	7	0.1667				No equation: all zero observations assumed to remain zero				
17	52	0.3846	0.4913	4	0.2245	$F_{(4,47)} = 3.40$[c]	0.4506	0.7570	1.8176	+1.0923,[f] -0.7630[g]
18	53	0.2453	0.4344	3	0.2135	$F_{(3,49)} = 4.43$[b]	0.3968	0.6666	0.3246	—
19	29	0.3448	0.4837	5	0.4636	$F_{(5,23)} = 3.98$[b]	0.3909	0.6700	0.6842	—

[a] Significant at a 0.001 test level.
[b] Significant at a 0.01 test level.
[c] Significant at a 0.025 test level.
[d] Discriminant cutoff equals (standard error of estimate) × (5% one-tail t-test level). The 5% one-tail test level is in the vicinity of 1.65 for large samples.
[e] Exceeds difference between discriminant cutoff and mean.
[f] Ln of total 1950 county employment in all industries.
[g] Ln of county population aged 21–64.

functions for industries 5 through 19. Columns (1) through (3) provide pretest data on the equations: the number of observations, and the means and standard deviations of the discriminant values. For instance, the mean of 0.2732 for industry 7 indicates the proportion of 1950 zero values which became nonzero in 1960. Column (4) gives the number of independent variables included in the final equations, while columns (5) through (7) provide the values of R^2, F, and the standard error of estimate. Despite the fact that the values of R^2 are very low, and that the standard errors are not reduced very much from the initial standard deviations, the correlations are generally highly significant according to an F-test criterion. In ten of the fourteen industries for which the discriminant functions were estimated, an F-test rejects the hypothesis that all coefficients were equal to zero at a 0.1 percent confidence level. Of the remaining four industries, three have correlations significant at a 1 percent test level, and the equation for industry 17 has a correlation significant at a 2.5 percent test level.

By observing the scale variable coefficients in column (10) of Table 6-2, and by observing the coefficient sign patterns in Table 6-3, we can make some observations about which county characteristics are associated with high discriminant scores. We must, however, reemphasize our caution against unthinkingly attributing a causal interpretation to the equations.

The first conclusion we can draw is that the larger is a county in population or employment size, the less likely it is to remain at zero employment in a given industry. In industries 5 through 13 we found a strong positive relationship between either lagged total employment or population aged 21–64 and a county's discriminant score. As our industry categories are relatively broad, it is extremely unlikely that a county with high total employment will have any zero industry observations. A scale variable is significant in each of these industries despite the fact that the discriminant score variable is itself scale free.

For industries 14 through 19 the pattern is less clear, with a negative sign in the equation for industry 15, and no significant coefficient in the equations for industries 18 and 19. The equations for industries 14 and 17 contain two scale variables (intercorrelated at a 0.98 correlation coefficient) with conflicting signs, indicating more the presence of serial correlation and an unstable relationship than anything else. In these industries the number of observations was small, only 78 and 52 counties respectively out of 3,097 in the country. The geometric mean of population in these counties aged 21–64 was about 1,200 per county, compared to over 10,000 per county for the nation as a whole (in 1950).

Certain other tendencies are apparent in the socioeconomic data: given the population size of a county, the discriminant score tends to rise with the rate of population growth and with proximity to SMSA's in excess

Table 6-3
Signs of Socioeconomic Variable Coefficients, First Discriminant Set*

Variables	5	6	7	8	9	10	11	12	13	14	15	17	18	19
115 Population, 1950/population, 1940	+					+					+			+
117 Population density					−		−							
118 Proportion population urban			+					+			+		+	
119 Proportion population rural farm			+											
120 Proportion population aged 21–64 years										+				
122 Births per family			−											
124 Proportion persons 25 years and over with less than 12 years education				+	+									+
126 Proportion labor force unemployed				+										
127 Proportion total employment in mining									−					
128 Proportion total employment in manufacturing		−												+
129 Proportion total employment in wholesale–retail trade					+									
130 Average family size										+				
131 Median family income			−			−		−				−	+	
133 Proportion dwelling units built after 1940						−								
134 Time and savings deposits/population					−									
136 Normal precipitation		−	+						+					
137 Distance to nearest SMSA with over 250,000 population								−					−	
138 Distance to nearest SMSA with over 1,000,000 population							−	−						
139 Terrain variability index										+				
140 Relative extent of unionization in state, 1940					−			+	+			−		+
142 Number of national highways		+	−						+	−				
143 Cost of oil		+			+									
144 Cost of gas														
145 Cost of electricity											+			
147 Median age														
148 Land area										+				
150 Employees per manufacturing establishment			+											−
168 Coefficient dummy for variable 123														

*See complete equations in Appendix D.

of 250,000 population. We found a surprising negative correlation with median family income. The gas cost variable (144) is positively correlated with employment in the three equations in which it appears, while the electricity cost variable (145) is negatively correlated in the three equations in which it appears. Other tendencies were scattered across industries, as indicated by the pattern of coefficient signs in Table 6–3.

While the discriminant functions are highly significant by standard test criteria, there is a serious question whether they can predict nonzero observations with any degree of power. Column (8) of Table 6–2 provides the discriminant score required to predict nonzero employment for 1960 (or 1970 in the prediction equations). Our criteria were discussed earlier: in order to predict a movement away from zero, we required the discriminant score to be significantly greater than zero at a 5 percent one-tail test level. If the number of observations is sufficiently large, the required discriminant cutoff is about 1.65 times the standard error of estimate. It is possible, of course, that no counties would be given a score which exceeds this cutoff.

The alternative to applying our discriminant function to a given industry is to apply the mean discriminant score to all counties, such as 0.1472 for industry 6. As 0.1472 is considerably less than the 0.5635 cutoff, that procedure would be tantamount to declaring all counties to remain at zero. The estimated equation distributes a set of discriminant scores with a smaller standard error than would the procedure of scoring each county with the value 0.1472. The range of scores, however, could conceivably be between, say, 0.1 and 0.2, in which case we would still fail to isolate any counties as being nonzero predictions.

To determine the power of each equation to produce discriminant scores in excess of the required cutoff, we observed that the beta weight of each right-hand variable indicates the number of standard deviations movement in the discriminant score associated with a one standard deviation movement in the right hand variable. Similarly, the sum of the absolute values of the beta weights, multiplied by the standard deviation of the discriminant score, represents the amount by which the discriminant score is increased by the movement of all variables by one standard deviation in the direction of improving that score. The larger is this potential movement, as measured by column (9), relative to the difference between the mean and the discriminant cutoff, the more likely are discriminant scores to be in excess of the cutoff. In only four of the fourteen equations does the beta weight "score" exceed this difference. In one of these four cases (industry 14) the absolute beta weight sum is misleading because of the presence of two highly correlated scale variables with opposite signs. Thus, while the discriminant functions are significant in a statistical sense, they do not appear to be performing their task effectively.

65

Discriminant Functions: Cases with
Nonzero Employment in 1950

As we have already stated, the second set of discriminant functions contained a much larger observation set than the first set. While less than 10 percent of counties with employment in a given industry in 1950 moved to the zero category in 1960, this movement in absolute terms was much larger than the opposite flow. As tables 6–4 and 6–5 show, this second set of discriminant functions performs very well compared to the first set.

The format of tables 6–4 and 6–5 is identical to that of tables 6–2 and 6–3. Columns (1) and (2) of table 6–4 support the statement made above concerning the larger number of observations and the larger percentage of nonzero discriminant scores. While an average of less than five variables per equation reduce the standard error of estimate in the first discriminant set, an average of almost eight variables per equation reduce the standard error in the second set. The values of R^2 again are rather low, but every equation passes an F-test at a 0.1 percent confidence level.

Column (8) gives the discriminant cutoffs calculated for each equation. Our criterion for predicting a zero value was, as described earlier, that the discriminant score be less than one at a 5 percent confidence level. With a large number of observations, the discriminant cutoff is therefore:

$$1 - 1.65 \cdot (\text{standard error of estimate})$$

where 1.65 is the approximate t-value required for a 5 percent one-tail test. In the previous section we discussed using the absolute sum of the beta weights multiplied by the standard deviation of the left hand variable as an indicator of an equation's power to predict zero values. In seven industries, compared to only four in the first discriminant set, this value exceeds the difference between the cutoff and the mean of the discriminant scores, although in two of the seven industries the presence of highly correlated scale variables with opposite signs contributes to the large beta weight value. Still, by this test, the second discriminant set is far superior to the first.

Not surprisingly, the estimated equations for virtually all industries display a strong positive correlation between discriminant scores and lagged scale variables. In thirteen out of fifteen industries lagged industry employment has a positive coefficient, indicating the rather obvious point that the larger is lagged employment, the less likely is a zero observation in the current period. More general size variables are also significant, as shown in column (11).

Relations to socioeconomic variables are more pronounced in the second discriminant set than in the first. There is an extremely powerful

Table 6-4
Results of Discriminant Functions, Nonzero Employment in 1950

	(1)	(2)	(3)	(4)	(5)	(6)	(7)	(8)	(9)	(10)	(11)
Industry Number	Number of Observations	Mean	Standard Deviation	Number of Right-hand Variables	R^2	F-statistic	Standard Error of Estimate	Discriminant Cutoff[b]	Absolute Sum of Beta Weights × Standard Deviation	Coefficient of Lagged Employment	Coefficient of Other Scale Variable
5	3019	0.9672	0.1781	6	0.1265	$F_{(6,3012)} = 72.67$[a]	0.1666	0.7251	0.1168	0.0380	–
6	2207	0.6733	0.4691	5	0.3213	$F_{(5,2201)} = 208.42$[a]	0.3869	0.3616	0.4115[c]	0.0853	0.0808[c]
7	2277	0.8630	0.3439	7	0.2914	$F_{(7,2269)} = 133.30$[a]	0.2900	0.5215	0.3922	0.0614	–
8	2917	0.9133	0.2815	5	0.3238	$F_{(5,2911)} = 278.81$[a]	0.2317	0.6177	0.2139	0.0701	–
9	3061	0.9526	0.2295	10	0.1215	$F_{(10,3050)} = 42.17$[a]	0.1995	0.6708	0.2295	–	0.0522[c]
10	2643	0.8138	0.3893	7	0.2194	$F_{(7,2635)} = 105.77$[a]	0.3444	0.4317	0.4033	0.0545	0.0445[d]
11	2886	0.9033	0.2956	10	0.1751	$F_{(10,2875)} = 61.02$[a]	0.2689	0.5563	0.3614	0.0229	0.0439[d]
12	2005	0.7172	0.4505	7	0.2727	$F_{(7,1997)} = 106.97$[a]	0.3848	0.3651	0.4951	0.0604	0.0874[d]
13	1877	0.7885	0.4085	6	0.1756	$F_{(6,1870)} = 66.41$[a]	0.3715	0.3870	0.2984	0.0593	–
14	3019	0.9503	0.2173	8	0.2039	$F_{(8,3010)} = 96.37$[a]	0.1942	0.6796	0.1834	0.0184	+.0063[d]
15	3037	0.9463	0.2254	7	0.2196	$F_{(7,3029)} = 121.79$[a]	0.1993	0.6712	0.2913	0.0837	–.0423[d]
16	3090	0.9783	0.1457	10	0.1123	$F_{(10,3079)} = 38.95$[a]	0.1375	0.7731	0.2011	–	–.1529[c], +.2347[c]
17	3045	0.9609	0.1938	7	0.1395	$F_{(7,3037)} = 70.33$[a]	0.1800	0.7030	0.4469	0.0298	–.1424[d], +.1362[c], +.0082[c]
18	3044	0.9428	0.2322	9	0.1632	$F_{(9,3034)} = 65.75$[a]	0.2127	0.6490	0.2482	0.0587	–
19	3068	0.9831	0.1291	11	0.1126	$F_{(11,3056)} = 35.26$[a]	0.1218	0.7990	0.1604	0.0366	–0.0151[c]

[a]Significant at a 0.001 test level.
[b]See footnote d, Table 6-2.
[c]Log of population aged 21–64.
[d]Log of total 1950 employment.
[e]Special transportation variable discussed in Chapter 5.

Table 6–5
Signs of Socioeconomic Variable Coefficients, Second Discriminant Set*

Variables	Industries														
	5	6	7	8	9	10	11	12	13	14	15	16	17	18	19
115 Population, 1950/population, 1940			+			+			+		+	+		+	+
116 Proportion population nonwhite	+			−				−						+	
117 Population density	−				−				−						−
118 Proportion population urban					+						+	+	−	+	+
119 Proportion population rural farm												−		−	−
120 Proportion population aged 21–64 years					−										
122 Births per family							−								
123 Proportion persons 25 years and over with less than 5 years education				+	+		+		+			+	−		+
124 Proportion persons 25 years and over with less than 12 years education										−	−	−	−		−
125 Proportion labor force male		−													
127 Proportion total employment in mining						+						+		+	
128 Proportion total employment in manufacturing									+						
129 Proportion total employment in wholesale-retail trade					+	+			+	+		+		+	−
130 Average family size	−		−	−		−	−	−		−			−		−
131 Median family income	+				+	−	+					+		+	
133 Proportion dwelling units built after 1940					+	−				+		+		+	
134 Time and savings deposits/population				−								+			
136 Normal precipitation	−								−						
137 Distance to nearest SMSA with over 250,000 population								+							
138 Distance to nearest SMSA with over 1,000,000 population		+	+		+			+				−			+
139 Terrain variability index											+				
140 Relative extent of unionization in state, 1940			+	−						+					
142 Number of national highways		+	+												
143 Cost of oil															
144 Cost of gas															
145 Cost of electricity															
147 Median age															
148 Land area															+
154 Intercept dummy for industry 11							−								
164 Coefficient dummy for variable 123							+								

*See Appendix D.

negative relationship between the discriminant score and the distance to an SMSA in excess of 250,000 population. There are rather consistent relationships between the discriminant score and the rate of population growth, the proportion employed in wholesale–retail trade, normal precipitation, the proportion of the population over 25 years of age with less than twelve years of education, and oil cost per barrel. There tends to be a negative relation with terrain variability and for industries 14 through 19 there is a negative correlation with the proportion of the population aged 21–64 and the proportion of the labor force which is male, and a positive correlation with the proportion of the population in rural and farm areas. The complete discriminant functions appear in Appendix D.

Regression Functions: Cases with
Zero Employment in 1950

The first set of regression functions was estimated for those counties which, for a given industry, had positive 1960 employment but zero 1950 employment. The purpose of these equations was to forecast 1970 employment for those counties predicted to move from zero in 1960 to positive employment in 1970. The first step of this procedure utilized the initial set of discriminant functions, which we noted to be somewhat substandard compared to the second set. Similarly, the first regression set leaves much to be desired, but the failure to find meaningful regressions may not be too damaging.

The results of the first regression set are presented in tables 6–6 and 6–7. By definition, none of the counties in this subset had lagged employment for use as a variable, although other scale variables were available. In half of the fourteen industries for which equations were estimated, the employment level is positively related to a scale variable.

There were more than 100 observations for only five equations. Five equations in all pass an F-test at a 0.1 percent significance level, including four of the five equations with more than 100 observations. The primary reason for our failure to find a well-fitting relationship may very well be that no such relationship exists. The logarithm means of the dependent variables ranged between 1.46 and 2.25, equivalent to a geometric mean ranging from 4.3 to 9.5 employees per county. This indicates that the typical county moving from zero to positive employment had an industry employment level of less than ten in the nonzero period. Given the small size of these counties, both the fact of movement to a nonzero level and the size of this movement may very well have had a large element which is legitimately random. This may be particularly true because our data are based on residence and not upon plant location.

We can therefore hypothesize that for the relatively broad industry

Table 6-6

Results of Regression Functions, Zero Employment in 1950, Nonzero Employment in 1960

Industry Number	(1) Number of Observations	(2) Mean	(3) Standard Deviation	(4) Number of Right-hand Variables	(5) R^2	(6) F-statistic	(7) Standard Error of Estimate	(8) Coefficient of Scale Variable
5	24	1.7256	0.4547	6	0.6417	$F_{(6,17)} = 5.08$[a]	0.3166	—
6	131	1.9000	0.9351	5	0.2142	$F_{(5,125)} = 6.81$[b]	0.8453	—
7	224	2.6511	1.4349	6	0.3648	$F_{(6,217)} = 20.77$[c]	1.1593	0.6087[c]
8	25	1.6177	0.4687	8	0.5840	$F_{(8,16)} = 2.81$[c]	0.3702	0.5240[c]
9	8	1.7918	0.4813	No equation: assign mean value to all counties passing discriminant score				
10	124	2.1027	1.0058	3	0.1349	$F_{(3,120)} = 6.24$[b]	0.9471	—
11	89	2.1082	0.8653	3	0.1531	$F_{(3,85)} = 5.12$[a]	0.8103	0.5881[c]
12	230	1.8410	0.6967	3	0.0298	$F_{(3,226)} = 2.31$[d]	0.6908	—
13	425	2.2473	1.0866	8	0.1116	$F_{(7,416)} = 6.53$[b]	1.0340	0.2021[c]
14	29	2.0207	0.6126	4	0.2590	$F_{(4,24)} = 2.10$	0.5696	0.5820[f]
15	3	1.4607	0.1288	1	0.9835	$F_{(1,1)} = 59.55$[d]	0.0234	−0.0904[c]
16	1	No equation						
17	20	1.8010	0.5914	4	0.3923	$F_{(4,15)} = 2.42$[d]	0.5189	0.1570[g]
18	13	1.5713	0.5109	4	0.9384	$F_{(4,8)} = 30.49$[b]	0.1552	0.7563[c]
19	10	1.8878	0.5099	2	0.5961	$F_{(2,7)} = 5.17$[c]	0.3674	—

[a] Significant at 0.0005 test level.
[b] Significant at 0.001 test level.
[c] Significant at 0.05 test level.
[d] Significant at 0.10 test level.
[e] Ln of total 1950 employment.
[f] Ln of population aged 21-64.
[g] Special transportation variable, described in Chapter 4.

Table 6–7
Signs of Socioeconomic Variable Coefficients, First Regression Set

#	Variables	\multicolumn{12}{c}{Industries}
		5	6	7	8	10	11	12	13	14	17	18	19
115	Population, 1950/population, 1940	+			+	+				−		+	
116	Proportion population nonwhite				−							−	
117	Population density						−					−	
118	Proportion population urban	−											
119	Proportion population rural farm	−		+	+			+	+			−	
122	Births per family					+							+
126	Proportion labor force unemployed	−											
127	Proportion total employment in mining				+								
128	Proportion total employment in manufacturing			+				+	+		+		
129	Proportion total employment in wholesale–retail trade					+		+	+				
131	Median family income			−			−						
133	Proportion dwelling units built after 1940								+	+			
135	Normal maximum temperature				+								
137	Distance to nearest SMSA with over 250,000 population				+				−	+	−		
138	Distance to nearest SMSA with over 1,000,000 population				+				+	+			
139	Terrain variability index				+					+			
140	Relative extent of unionization in state, 1940		−										
142	Number of national highways		+	+							+		
143	Cost of oil	+	+										
144	Cost of gas		+					+					
145	Cost of electricity	+			+								
148	Land area	+											
150	Employees per manufacturing establishment			+									−
165	Coefficient dummy for variable 123								−				

classifications which we are using, the zero status of a county is to a large extent a random occurrence which becomes less likely as the absolute size of a county's population increases. There is some size at which the probability of a zero observation in *any* of our industries becomes effectively zero. As an extreme instance, whatever our conception may be of New York County (Manhattan) as a strictly urban county, it does *not* have literally zero employment in agriculture (569) or forestry and fisheries (35).

As we were restricting ourselves in this set of equations to those counties which moved from literally zero employment to a positive level of employment, our sample set was a heterogeneous mixture of counties which had either a trivially random movement from zero to, say, three, or a significant movement from zero to some number which was large relative to the county size. Furthermore, counties which moved from some trivially small employment rate to a far greater rate were omitted altogether from our discriminant analysis (and first regression set). Such counties were instead in the second regression set, which included a vast majority of the counties. In the converse case a county with a movement from high employment to a trivially small level would have been assigned a positive score in the second discriminant set.

This raises the question as to whether it would have been wiser to have chosen some point other than zero to distinguish between significant and insignificant employment levels. Such a procedure might have worked, but the arbitrariness of such a cutoff would have raised many of the same problems, unless a band of counties on the margin were explicitly omitted from the analysis. Such a possibility was overridden by our need to include an exhaustive set of counties in our analysis, and by our a priori suspicion that in many cases the presence of a zero observation may have more significance than its random difference from a number such as one or two.

It was felt that the weakness of this link would be relatively unimportant. First, it was considered likely that a county which moved from zero to a high employment level would still be selected by the first discriminant function–regression sequence, for extreme observations usually do "much of the work" in determining regression coefficients. Second, if a movement from zero to four is truly random, it should not make too much difference whether, on the one hand, the county fails the discriminant test and is predicted to have zero employment, or, on the other hand, passes the discriminant test and is assigned some small employment value.

In the estimated equations, population growth, proportion of population rural-farm, proportion employed in manufacturing, and normal maximum temperature are all generally positively correlated with employment in the first regression set. No other variables appear in the equations for more than two industries.

Regression Functions: Counties with
Continuing Positive Employment

The second regression set includes the vast majority of counties which had positive employment for a given industry in both 1950 and 1960. Because of inertial factors the prior existence of an industry in an area tends to increase the likelihood of that industry's continued existence. For this reason the availability of lagged employment as a variable improved the fit of our regressions considerably.

Tables 6–8 and 6–9 present the basic data for this regression set. Of the twenty industries for which equations were estimated, thirteen industries had continuing positive employment in at least 92 percent of the counties of the contiguous United States. The seven industries which were not so commonly present were textiles, apparel, lumber and wood products, chemicals, machinery, motor vehicles, and other transportation equipment. As columns (5) and (6) indicate, the equations for these seven industries performed worst in terms of goodness of fit.

These same seven industries (6 through 8 and 10 through 13) were also becoming more concentrated in two senses. First, as shown in Table 6–1 the number of counties in which each of these industries appears diminished in every instance except industry 13. Second, among the subset of counties with continuing positive employment, the distribution of employment became more concentrated in the sense that the logarithmic standard deviation fell between 1950 and 1960. An examination of columns (3) and (9) in Table 6–8 can verify this observation.

The equations for the remaining thirteen industries perform far better in terms of R^2 F, and the standard error of estimate. Furthermore, we were generally able to find more statistically significant explanatory variables for the former thirteen industries than for the latter seven.

Columns (10) and (11) present the coefficients of the scale variables. While in most cases the sum of the coefficients is quite close to one in value, we must emphasize the clear presence of an aggregation problem. While we anticipated this in Chapter 4, there is no effective way of dealing with the problem except to warn of its existence. In eighteen of the twenty industries, we found scale variables which remained significant in the presence of lagged industry employment. These coefficients are reported in column (11), and test statistics for all coefficients appear in Appendix D.

Table 6–9 presents a tabular summary of the signs of the socioeconomic variables as they appear in the regressions. As we found in the previous regression sets, the rate of population growth (variable 115) has a very strong positive impact on employment location. The distance to SMSA's with populations exceeding 250,000 has a fairly strong negative impact on a large number of industries. In nine industries, a high proportion of the population engaged in mining is associated with smaller

Table 6-8
Results of Regression Functions, Nonzero Employment, 1950 and 1960

Industry Number	(1) Number of Observations	(2) Mean	(3) Standard Deviation	(4) Number of Right-hand Variables	(5) R^2	(6) F-statistic[a]	(7) Standard Error of Estimate	(8) Mean	(9) Standard Deviation	(10) Coefficient	(11) Coefficient of Other Scaled Variable
								1950 Employment			
1	3097	6.8314	.9922	19	0.9195	$F_{(19,3077)}=1849.35$	0.2824	7.3851	0.9230	0.9575	0.165[b]
4	3097	6.0542	1.2914	12	0.9366	$F_{(12,3084)}=3796.77$	0.3258	5.9854	1.2331	0.7038	0.2761[c]
5	2920	4.8886	1.6806	12	0.8896	$F_{(12,2907)}=1951.48$	0.5596	4.4366	1.7410	0.7338	0.3258[d]
6	1486	4.1307	2.2528	7	0.7898	$F_{(7,1478)}=793.51$	1.0352	3.9865	2.5889	0.7200	0.1886[d]
7	1965	4.6259	1.7729	9	0.7224	$F_{(9,1955)}=565.30$	0.9362	3.7651	2.1758	0.6297	0.3997[d]
8	2664	4.8789	1.6112	8	0.8669	$F_{(8,2655)}=2162.08$	0.5886	4.9533	1.7102	0.8599	—
9	2916	4.0430	1.6669	10	0.9085	$F_{(10,2905)}=2885.64$	0.5050	3.6662	1.6486	0.5950	0.4156[c]
10	2151	3.8600	1.9012	6	0.7087	$F_{(6,2144)}=869.15$	1.0276	3.3934	2.0172	0.6669	—
11	2607	4.5084	2.1545	9	0.8419	$F_{(9,2597)}=1536.45$	0.8582	3.6640	2.2305	0.6723	0.3510[c]
12	1438	3.6161	1.9770	8	0.7690	$F_{(8,1429)}=594.57$	0.9529	2.9672	2.2584	0.6890	0.2596[c]
13	1480	3.9971	1.9699	7	0.6773	$F_{(7,1472)}=441.34$	1.1217	2.5960	2.1749	0.6212	0.2867[c]
14	2869	5.3666	2.0805	11	0.8816	$F_{(11,2857)}=1933.08$	0.7174	4.8163	2.2424	0.7568	0.2719[c]
15	2874	4.2368	1.6086	9	0.9159	$F_{(9,2864)}=3466.78$	0.4672	4.7173	1.5524	0.9290	0.0787[c]
16	3023	4.4257	1.4057	13	0.8858	$F_{(13,3009)}=1794.52$	0.4761	4.2501	1.3092	0.6207	0.2674[d] 0.1285[c]
17	2926	3.9532	1.4528	8	0.8627	$F_{(8,2917)}=2291.08$	0.5391	3.8211	1.5398	0.6226	0.2858[c] 0.0706[c]
18	2870	4.1208	1.5362	12	0.8905	$F_{(12,2857)}=1936.04$	0.5094	3.9893	1.4916	0.6019	0.3846[d]
19	3016	4.4509	1.4229	7	0.8977	$F_{(7,3008)}=3772.57$	0.4555	4.2444	1.4425	0.7033	0.2767[d]
20	3097	7.4640	1.3623	14	0.9638	$F_{(14,3082)}=5864.84$	0.2597	7.2822	1.3601	0.2353[f]	0.7751[d,f]
21	3097	6.7011	1.3790	11	0.9784	$F_{(11,3085)}=12674.29$	0.2033	6.3996	1.2931	0.8723	0.1171[c]
22	3097	5.5481	1.3295	14	0.9496	$F_{(14,3082)}=4145.42$	0.2992	5.3148	1.2799	0.8855	0.1033[c]

[a] All significant at 0.001 test level.
[b] Special agricultural variable discussed in Chapter 4.
[c] Ln of population aged 21-64.
[d] Ln of total 1950 employment.
[e] Special transportation variable, discussed in special industry chapter.
[f] Industry 20 erroneously regressed against lagged employment for industry 21. The predictive power is not significantly altered, however, since E_{50}^{20} and E_{50}^{21} have a zero order correlation coefficient of 0.975 and E total/50 also have a zero order correlation of 0.975. Note that E total/50 takes up the slack left by the ommission of the proper lagged employment variable.

74

Table 6–9
Signs of Socioeconomic Variable Coefficients, Second Regression Set

	Variable	1	4	5	6	7	8	9	10	11	12	13	14	15	16	17	18	19	20	21	22
115	Population, 1950/population, 1940	+	+	+			+	+	+	+		+	+	+	+		+			+	+
116	Proportion population nonwhite	−		−		−															
117	Population density	+		−													−		+		
118	Proportion population urban	+															+		−		
119	Proportion population rural farm			+			+	−		+	−	+	−	−	−		+		+		
120	Proportion population aged 21–64 years			+		−		−		+		+					−				+
122	Births per family			+		−		−													
123	Proportion persons 25 years and over with less than 5 years education					+							+			+				+	+
124	Proportion persons 25 years and over with less than 12 years education					+				−			+	−		+				+	+
125	Proportion labor force male	+						−						−	−				−	−	−
126	Proportion labor force unemployed			−		−				−	−			−	−			−	−	−	
127	Proportion total employment in mining	−		−									−		+	−			+	−	+
128	Proportion total employment in manufacturing	−	+	−					+					−	+	−			−	+	−

#	Variable																		
129	Proportion total employment in wholesale–retail trade		+		−	−				−	+		+			+		+	
130	Average family size	−																	+
131	Median family income	+	−	−							+			−					
133	Proportion dwelling units built after 1940	−	+			−						+	+	+	+	+			
134	Time and savings deposits/population	+			−	−							+					+	
135	Normal maximum temperature				−						+		+			+		+	
136	Normal precipitation		+					+									+		
137	Distance to nearest SMSA with over 250,000 population	+	−		−	−	−	−	−		+		−		−	−	−		
138	Distance to nearest SMSA with over 1,000,000 population	+	+							−		+							
139	Terrain variability index	−		−	+	−										−			
140	Relative extent of unionization in state, 1940							+											
142	Number of national highways				+		+												
143	Cost of oil	−		+	−		+	+					−			−			
144	Cost of gas	+	+		+	+													
145	Cost of electricity		+		−	+			+				+	+		+	+		
147	Median age							+											
148	Land area												+		+				
152	Intercept dummy for industry 5			+															
159	Intercept dummy for industry 14									+									
168	Coefficient dummy for variable 123									−									

employment in 1960. Employment in industries 16–20 (transportation, communications, utilities, and population-oriented services) is positively related to the proportion of dwelling units built since 1940. Proportion of population over 25 years of age with less than twelve years of education is in general negatively correlated with employment, as is the proportion of the labor force unemployed and normal maximum temperature. Gas cost and electricity cost, on the other hand, are positively correlated with employment in those equations in which they appear. Other variables are somewhat less systematic in their correlations.

Discussion of Individual Variables

In general it would be unwise to attempt to derive cause-and-effect relationships from our results. One can only say that in the past a particular variable has been associated with a particular employment rate, holding the values of all other explanatory variables constant. If such associations will remain constant in the future, then we can make predictions of employment by observing the current values of the socioeconomic variables.

The most effective variable was population growth (115), which was, with only one exception, positively associated with employment in the regression and the discriminant equations in which it appeared. This variable appears in equations for both manufacturing and service industries. In the R_2 equations, the coefficient of this variable ranges from 0.2 for railroads (15) to 0.9 for chemicals (10), with the average value of the coefficient being about 0.5. In other words, using the average coefficient value of 0.5, a doubling of population growth indicates that the *logarithm* of future employment will increase by one (0.5 times 2), or that the value of future employment will be, other things equal, 2.72 times larger than the value of present employment. Thus, those counties with a high growth in population in the past are likely to exhibit a high growth in employment in the future.

Distance to nearest SMSA with a population greater than 250,000 also appears in more than half the equations, including both manufacturing and service industry equations. (This variable is similar to the population density variable that Fuchs found was correlated with employment.) As expected, this variable was in general negatively correlated with employment—it appears with a positive sign in only two equations. This variable appears more often than any other variable in the discriminant equations. The value of the slope coefficient in the R_2 equations varies from −0.0003 in population-oriented services (21) to −0.003 in other transportation equipment (13). Thus, using −0.001 as the average coefficient, an increase of 1,000 miles in the distance from a large SMSA is needed to decrease the logarithm of employment by 1, and the effect is therefore relatively weak. Curiously, distance to an SMSA with a population greater than one million (variable 138) enters few equations, and often with the wrong sign. Variable 138 enters eight equations in all, and in five cases the sign is perverse. Thus, there appear to be external economies from being near a small city, but as the size of the city approaches a population of one million these external economies diminish.

Variable 127 (proportion employed in mining) appears in ten R_2 equations, although it only appears once in each of the other sets of equations. Except for the equation for industry 16, mining employment was negatively correlated with employment. However, as we have stated above, the reason for the negative correlation is undoubtedly that mining-intensive counties possess a constellation of socioeconomic characteristics that contribute to economic stagnation and which we have been unable to identify with the other variables.

Variables 128 and 129 (proportion employed in manufacturing and proportion employed in wholesale–retail) each appear in eight R_2 equations. These two variables also appear in a number of D_2 and R_1 equations, though each appears only once in the D_1 equations. However, no clear pattern can be discerned among the coefficients.

The results for the three fuel and power cost variables, 143, 144, and 145 (oil cost, gas cost, and electricity cost) illustrate the simultaneous equation bias present in our system. These three variables appear often in the equations.[2] The interesting fact is that more often than not these variables appear with a positive sign — that is, greater fuel costs are associated with higher levels of employment. Obviously we are not observing the true causal sequence — we cannot conclude that we can increase employment by increasing fuel or power costs. We are in fact probably observing two offsetting tendencies: lower fuel or power costs would be an incentive for greater employment, but on the other hand greater employment in an area would tend to drive up fuel and power costs.

A number of the intercept and slope dummies are significant in the equations for industries 5, 11, 13, and 14, indicating that these industries are not homogeneous. For example, variable 152 (state proportion of industry 5 in canning) has a positive coefficient of 0.6 in the R_2 equation for industry 5, indicating that there was an upward shift of the entire function for industry 5 for states which have a high proportion of canning in industry 5. Similarly, variable 159 (state proportion of industry 14 in metal manufacturing) has a negative coefficient in the R_2 equation for industry 14, indicating that the functional relationships for metal manu-

---

[2] In the R_2 equations variable 143 appears seven times, variable 144 appears four times, and variable 145 appears eight times; in the D_1 equations variable 143 appears once, variable 144 appears three times, and variable 145 appears three times; in the D_2 equations variable 143 appears three times, variable 144 appears twice, and variable 145 appears twice; and in the R_1 equations variable 143 appears twice, variable 144 appears once, and variable 145 appears twice.

facturing differ from those for other industry 14 activities. Again, the presence of variable 168 (proportion heavy industry in industry 14 × proportion education $<$ 5 years) in the R_2 and D_1 equations for industry 14 indicates that the effect of the educational level of the population on employment is different for heavy industry than it is for other industry 14 activities.

The results for other variables are so mixed that it is difficult to derive any pattern. In general, therefore, we found that location near a center of population with greater than 250,000 but fewer than one million people has a strong positive effect on industrial growth, and that the size variables (lagged total employment, lagged population and lagged industry employment) have strong positive effects on future employment. Economies of scale and external economies therefore appear to be key factors in industrial growth. Furthermore, counties which have exhibited a large growth of population in the past tend to have large growths of employment in future decades.[3]

Projections of Employment

As mentioned above, certain corrections were made in the regression equations before they were used in the projection analysis. In particular, in order to correct for the bias of using absolute cross-section regression coefficients of variables which are significant only in determining relative county orderings (see Chapter 3) we assumed that only the scale variables (lagged employment and size of labor force) have an absolute effect on employment. All other variables were assumed to be relative variables, and therefore were adjusted in proportion to their respective increases or decreases in the country as a whole between 1950 and 1960. It should be pointed out that the mean value in the United States as a whole for a particular variable often differed considerably from the mean of the values for all counties. Such an anomaly may arise because the distribution of counties is not random—for example, the percentage of counties that are rural is far higher than the percentage of employment in rural areas. Presumably, however, relative variables should be interpreted in relation to a national norm.

We therefore multiplied the coefficient of every relative variable by the ratio of the national mean in 1960 to the national mean in 1950. These

---

[3] It is interesting to note that the "relative degree of unionization" and "climate," which were found by Fuchs to be significantly related to employment, were not consistently correlated with employment in our equations. In addition, "availability of skills," which Chinitz and Vernon concluded was highly correlated with growth in industrial employment, was also not consistently correlated with employment in our equations (as measured by the education variables).

weighting factors are given in Table 6–10. The actual equations used for the forecasts are presented in Appendix E.

Table 6–10

Industry Adjustment Factors

	Industry	Adjustment Factor
1.	Agriculture	0.73265
2.	Forestry and fisheries	1.0202
3.	Mining	0.76493
4.	Contract construction	1.24268
5.	Food and kindred products	1.10888
6.	Textiles	0.93628
7.	Apparel	1.13055
8.	Lumber, wood, and furniture	1.01911
9.	Printing and publishing	1.13787
10.	Chemical and allied products	0.94929
11.	Machinery	1.19911
12.	Motor vehicles and equipment	1.02018
13.	Other transportation equipment	0.98224
14.	Miscellaneous manufacturing	1.13968
15–17.	Transportation	0.9705
18.	Communications	0.867333
19.	Utilities	0.92136
20.	Consumer services	1.24575
21.	Business and professional services	1.55956
22.	Public administration	1.4802
23.	Armed Forces	1.00000
24.	Industry not reported	1.19459

In general the projected employments by industry for each county appear to be quite satisfactory—at least the 1970 county employments are almost always of the same magnitude as the 1960 employments. Furthermore, implied state growth rates seem to accord well with a priori expectations (see Table 6–11). For example, the three states with the largest projected growths were Florida (60 percent), Arizona (57 percent), and California (40 percent), while the five states with the smallest projected growths were West Virginia (−4 percent), Montana (1 percent), Mississippi (2 percent), North Dakota (2 percent), and South Dakota (2 percent).

While the overall projections are satisfactory, the model made poor projections in several cases. For example, we projected employment in industry 17 (other transportation) in Buena Vista City, Virginia to grow from 0 in 1960 to 481,012 in 1970. The reason for this was that the R_1 equation for industry 17 had a very high coefficient (22.5517) for variable 128 (proportion employed in manufacturing). While all of the counties that went from zero employment in 1950 to positive employment in 1960

Table 6-11

Projected State Employment Growth Rates

State	Growth Rate of Total Employment	State	Growth Rate of Total Employment
Alabama	9%	Montana	1%
Arizona	47	Nebraska	11
Arkansas	0	Nevada	22
California	40	New Hampshire	11
Colorado	36	New Jersey	22
Connecticut	23	New Mexico	35
Delaware	25	New York	12
District of Columbia	25	North Carolina	9
Florida	60	North Dakota	2
Georgia	14	Ohio	20
Idaho	6	Oklahoma	13
Illinois	16	Oregon	14
Indiana	15	Pennsylvania	11
Iowa	8	Rhode Island	13
Kansas	18	South Carolina	9
Kentucky	5	South Dakota	2
Louisiana	15	Tennessee	10
Maine	3	Texas	19
Maryland	34	Utah	27
Massachusetts	19	Vermont	3
Michigan	19	Virginia*	23
Minnesota	15	Washington	13
Mississippi	2	West Virginia	−4
Missouri	15	Wisconsin	12
		Wyoming	3

*Adjusted to compensate for an error in the projection of industry 17 (other transportation).

in industry 17 had a low proportion of manufacturing employment, employment in 1960 was strongly correlated with this proportion, and therefore the slope coefficient of variable 128 was very high. Unfortunately, Buena Vista City, whose equation has a high value for variable 128, was picked by the discriminant equation to have positive employment. Therefore, when the R_1 equation was applied to this county, the estimated employment was absurdly large.

As the projections were scaled so that their sums would equal Almon's projections, there is no easy way to correct for errors of this nature. An overestimate of employment in an industry in one county means that employment in that industry in all other counties will be underestimated. The example of Buena Vista City cited above is the worst overestimate we were able to find in the projections. However, we also found three other grossly overestimated projections:

County	Industry	1960 Employment (Actual)	1970 Employment (Projected)
Alpine, California	Utilities	0	109,239
Brevard, Florida	Chemicals	35	1,679
Schley, Georgia	Other transportation	0	3,444

Two of these implausible projections are caused by R_1 equations (for counties predicted to pass from zero employment in 1960 to positive employment in 1970).

In addition to the overestimates resulting primarily from the R_1 equations, the model in several instances substantially underestimated 1970 employment in the home counties of highly concentrated industries. For example, employment in industry 12 (motor vehicles) in Michigan was projected to decrease from 377,163 in 1960 to 229,554 in 1970. The declines projected for counties with a large 1960 employment in motor vehicles are given below:

County	1960 Employment (Actual)	1970 Employment (Projected)	Percent Decline
Genessee	54,900	28,029	48%
Ingham	12,081	8,402	29
Macomb	24,222	14,236	40
Oakland	48,801	28,610	40
Saginaw	8,340	5,990	27
Wayne	173,428	89,244	48

These obviously inaccurate results are undoubtedly caused by the fact that in the equation for industry 12 we were unable to account sufficiently for such things as decision-making inertia and economies of scale. In all probability there is nothing in Genessee, Ingham, Macomb, Oakland, Saginaw, and Wayne counties which makes them uniquely suitable for being the centers of the automobile industry other than that, partly because of historical accident, the automobile industry has been concentrated there in the past. Given this concentration, however, these counties are able to retain employment in automobile manufacturing, partly because of decision-making inertia, partly because of the high costs of moving elsewhere, partly because of economies of scale, and partly because of the external economies arising from other industries which have been attracted to these counties (or to neighboring counties) by the presence of the automobile industry. As there is no reason to believe that the counties mentioned would be inferior, all else being equal, to other counties for automobile manufacturing, the latter two reasons are probably the most important. In our equations we tried to account for the economies of agglomeration mentioned above by the use of lagged employment as an explanatory variable. Apparently, however, this variable was not powerful enough to pick up all the effects of agglomeration economies.

When one considers, however, that our model generated 74,328 separate employment projections (24 industries in 3,097 counties) it is remarkable how few implausible projections were made. Of course, because of reasons such as the ones discussed above, the projections for any one county may be inaccurate; such an outcome is inevitable given the nature of our task.

Appendixes

Appendix A

The National Employment Forecasts

A major task of this study is to analyze the relative attractiveness of an area for the location of an industry. Our approach to this problem has been to project growth in employment by industry by county. However, our basic unadjusted employment model does not take into account national macroeconomic growth relationships.

We therefore scaled the county employment projections so that they summed to an internally consistent set of national industry employment forecasts. Forecasting total national production by industry represents a formidable task. Fortunately, a study of this nature has already been performed by Professor Clopper Almon, Jr.[1] Essentially, he uses input–output analysis to project the rate of growth of output and of employment of 90 industries by year from 1964 to 1975.

Almon's model satisfies three essential criteria for our project:

1. It makes detailed industry projections over several years for the United States economy as a whole.
2. Its projections are based on reasonable assumptions and can be examined for their sensitivity to the assumptions.
3. It is internally consistent.

Brief Description of Input–Output Analysis

It would be inappropriate to present a detailed description of input–output analysis in this book. However, for the benefit of nontechnical readers it may be useful to summarize briefly its essential features.

An input–output table is simply an accounting device that states exactly the inputs necessary to produce a given set of final demands. The table below shows how an input–output table for a simple economy consisting of two intermediate products (steel and cement), one final product (consumer goods), and one factor of production (labor) might appear.

Buyer Seller	(1) Steel	(2) Cement	(3) Consumer Goods
(1) Steel	a_{11}	a_{12}	a_{13}
(2) Cement	a_{21}	a_{22}	a_{23}
(3) Labor	a_{31}	a_{32}	a_{33}

---

[1] We utilized Professor Almon's unpublished working papers, but most of his conclusions are available in Clopper Almon, Jr., *The American Economy to 1975 — An Interindustry Forecast* (New York: Harper & Row, 1966).

The coefficients a_{ij} in the table represent the quantity of product i needed to produce a unit of product j (the a_{ij} are commonly referred to as technological coefficients). For example, defining a unit to be one dollar's worth of product, one dollar's worth of cement requires a_{12} dollars of steel, a_{22} dollars of cement, and a_{32} dollars of labor. Thus, an input–output table takes into account all intermediate product relationships.

An input–output table can be used to calculate the total production of goods required to obtain a given quantity of final products. For example, the total quantity of steel (X_1), cement (X_2), and labor (L) required to produce X_3 units of consumer goods can be calculated by solving the following system of equations:

$$X_1 = a_{11}X_1 + a_{12}X_2 + a_{13}X_3 \qquad (A.1)$$

$$X_2 = a_{21}X_1 + a_{22}X_2 + a_{23}X_3 \qquad (A.2)$$

$$L = a_{31}X_1 + a_{32}X_3 + a_{33}X_3 \qquad (A.3)$$

As described so far, there is no mechanism in input–output analysis to ensure that the pattern of final demand for goods will be consistent with the level of factor inputs available in the economy. Almon makes the reasonable assumption that the government will regulate the economy in such a way as to ensure a full-employment final demand.

Input–output analysis has a number of drawbacks, as one would expect of so ambitious a technique; in particular:

1. There is no supply equation for factors of production. Input–output analysis, in effect, usually assumes a fixed supply of factors, although this assumption is theoretically unnecessary. There is probably a positive elasticity in the supply of labor, but the magnitude of this elasticity is an open question.

2. Input–output analysis assumes constant-coefficient production functions. By making this assumption, input–output analysis rules out all externalities and all economies or diseconomies of scale. There is no empirical evidence to justify this assumption, but over sufficiently small ranges the assumption of constant coefficients will provide a good approximation to the true relationship.

3. Input–output data must be measured at a discrete point of time, and there is no guarantee that the economy is in an equilibrium state at this observed moment. That is, the coefficients observed may not be the true long-run coefficients. Furthermore, as input–output analysis assumes equilibrium, it has no mechanism for predicting fluctuations in inventories. If the level of inventories in the economy is not at an equilibrium at the time the input–output table is calculated, projections made with the table will be incorrect.

4. A serious aggregation problem is also inherent in input–output analysis. Each industry sector in any feasible model is an aggregation

of many smaller industries. It is generally known that exact linear aggregation of nonlinear functions is impossible in general. Therefore, for the aggregation problem to be fully tractable, all production functions must be linear. Furthermore, if the linear production functions vary among subindustries, the coefficients will not be meaningful unless the percentage compositions of the sectors of the model are invariant over time.

5. Input–output analysis is forced to assume that all sectors pay the same price for their inputs, as input–output data are collected in value terms. Without the assumption of equal prices, there would be no guarantee that the sum of the entries across a row would equal the total value of the product; even if this occurred, no meaningful interpretation could be given the individual entries without information on the prices each sector paid for its inputs.

6. Input–output analysis assumes all elasticities of substitution on the input side are equal to zero.

7. The treatment of investment in input–output analysis is also unsatisfactory. Most models either treat investment as an exogenous final demand or assume that investment is a fixed proportion of production.

8. The concept of a production function is probably not very meaningful for such sectors as agriculture, retail trade, foreign trade, government, finance, and other service sectors. There is no reason for believing that outputs are proportional to inputs in these sectors.

9. Input–output analysis also does not distinguish among supplies of different types of factors. For example, in the Almon model labor is assumed to be homogeneous. Unfortunately, because of data inadequacies most empirical models must make this assumption.

It should be understood, of course, that the above listing of drawbacks is not meant to imply that input–output analysis should be rejected, for oversimplified assumptions are necessary for almost all economic analysis. Input–output analysis, properly applied, is indeed an extremely useful tool of economic analysis, and we intend only to suggest that the results of input–output analysis should be qualified in the light of the drawbacks inherent in the technique itself.

Description of the Almon Model

Almon used a ninety-sector input–output matrix based on 1958 data. As this year was a recession year, the technological coefficients measured for the year may not be representative of those for "normal" years; but 1958 was the most recent year available for his study.

For any year, Almon assumed that a certain percentage of the labor force is employed. For example, the figure in 1970 is 96 percent (this is really making an assumption about government fiscal policy). The question to be answered is what amounts of final demand and investment demand are required to generate a total production figure that exactly uses the specified percentage of the expected labor force. The Almon solution employs a six-step iteration.

1. The first step is the projection of government expenditures for the products of the ninety industries. Three types of government expenditures were distinguished: defense, general federal, and state and local. It was assumed that purchases by state and local governments from all industries would grow at a rate of 4.1 percent per year and that general federal purchases from all industries would grow at 4 percent per year. The defense final demand was assumed to remain at approximately the 1964 rate (this assumption has turned out to be too low).

2. A trial projection is then made of disposable income per capita, and consumer expenditures per person for the products of each industry are calculated, using a preestimated consumption function. Multiplying these per capita expenditures by the expected population gives total consumer demand for the products of each industry.

3. Spending for construction, investment, and inventory accumulation by each industry are then estimated by applying a preestimated capital investment function to a trial projection of industrial production.

4. Using the input–output table, the gross production in each industry necessary to sustain the initial estimates of demand for final goods is calculated.

5. If estimated production in any industry is greater than that assumed in step 4, this step is then recalculated using the new production figures. This procedure is repeated until consistency is obtained.

6. When the results of step 4 and step 5 are consistent, the output figures are then used to derive the employment requirements for the various industries. If the total is exactly equal to the specified percentage of the labor force, the problem is solved. If not—for example, if labor required is greater than labor available—a new estimate of disposable income must be made. In this case, the original estimate would be reduced. Steps 1–6 would then be repeated.

This analysis is then repeated for every year of the forecast period. Almon adjusted his input–output table for each year of his study to take into account expected changes in the technological coefficients. This adjustment, which by necessity is approximate, takes into account the introduction of known techniques as new investments are made, projections of trends that existed in the 1950s, expected product mix changes within industry categories, and wherever possible the effects of expected changes in relative prices.

One of the most important advantages of input–output analysis as used by Almon is not that it provides a better tool for making projections of final demand, but that it provides a way of examining the implications of these projections for particular producing industries. For instance, it is not difficult to predict that increasing income and leisure time will have a salutary effect on sales of sporting goods, but it is less clear what effect increased sporting goods sales will have on the sales of electricity, petroleum, structural steel, and metal fabricating machinery, unless one has spelled out the economy's industrial relationships in the detail that an input–output analysis can provide. The projections for output are only as good as the projections for final demand and for the coefficients in the matrix, but they are likely to be better than output forecasts that do not systematically take account of the interdependences in the economy. We now turn to the specific assumptions Almon used in making his projections.

Discussion of the Almon Data and Assumptions

The input–output matrix used in Almon's study contains ninety industries, final demand sectors, and a labor force. The ninety industries sell goods and services for inputs for other current production, for capital investment, and for final demand. As purchasers, the ninety industries buy intermediate goods and employ labor. The capital goods are sold to a smaller number of capital purchasing sectors, each sector being an aggregation of several of the ninety industries and employing no labor. The final demand sectors purchase all the goods and services not purchased by producing industries and also employ no labor. The final demand sectors are exports, state and local government, the federal government, and consumers.

The ninety industries are the same as the eighty-six industry categories used by the Office of Business Economics for the 1958 Interindustry Study, with three exceptions.[2] OBE's food-and-kindred-products group is disaggregated into seven components and the electric, gas, water, and sanitary services group into three components. The scrap industry is not included. Government industry, rest of the world industry, and household industry are eliminated from the producing sectors and treated only as purchasers of final output.

The accounting conventions and the 1958 input–output data were also taken almost entirely from the OBE data. Since economic data for 1963 were available at the time of the study, the 1958 input–output table was applied to the 1963 base data. Corrections were made in the input–output coefficients wherever possible. The 1963 output and employment figures for each industry were arrived at by applying actual 1963 total labor force,

---

[2] N. R. Goldman, M. L. Marimont, and B. N. Vaccara, "The Interindustry Structure of the United States," *Survey of Current Business* 44, No. 11 (November 1964): 10–29.

disposable income, government expenditure, and foreign trade figures to the matrix of estimated 1963 coefficients.

Two sectors of the model, foreign trade and population and labor force, were treated outside of the model. The population forecast was made by accepting the second highest of the four alternative projections made by the U.S. Census Bureau for U.S. population. Exports were basically treated by projecting recent trends. Imports were treated in two ways. Imports of goods not produced in the United States were treated as a producing row in the input–output matrix and consequently the amounts of these "noncompetitive" imports were determined in the solution of the matrix. Imports that are directly competitive with domestic commodities of the same types appear in the input–output table as negative entries in an import column, where they reduce the total demand for the corresponding domestically produced commodity. They were treated as negative exports and were independently projected. Crude petroleum, iron and nonferrous metal ores, raw sugar, textiles, lumber, newsprint, refined metals, and machinery and instruments account for the bulk of these competitive imports. The future rates of growth of these imports were projected to be the same as the rates of growth of the domestic counterparts.

**Use of the Almon Forecasts
in Our Projections**

Almon presents his results in terms of growth rates of employment in the ninety sectors of his model. These growth rates were converted to estimates of employment in 1970 of the twenty-four sectors of our model.

In order to make the projections comparable to the census data used in our study, we applied the Almon growth rates to 1960 data to obtain the 1970 projections. However, we were not able to use his growth rates directly as his sectors do not correspond exactly to ours. In all cases except for the transportation sectors, our industry sectors are composed of several Almon industries. Fortunately, in no case does an Almon industry belong to more than one of our industries.

Using the Almon growth rate projections, we were, therefore, able to obtain weighted growth rates which could be applied to our industries. The procedure we used was as follows:

1. Determine the Almon industries corresponding to a particular CRA industry.
2. Find the 1960 employment corresponding to each Almon industry from *Employment and Earnings Statistics,* the principal data source used by Almon.

3. Project 1970·employment for each Almon industry from step 1 on the basis of the 1960 employments found in step 2 and Almon's growth rates.
4. Sum the 1960 employments and the 1970 employments corresponding to the CRA industry in question and calculate the ratio of 1970 employment to 1960 employment.
5. Apply this ratio to the 1960 employment data used in our model.

The last two steps were necessary because the employment rates published in *Employment and Earnings Statistics* are not completely comparable to the 1960 census employment rates used in our model. Special assumptions had to be made for two industries in our model: Armed Forces (23) and industry not reported (24). We assumed that Armed Forces employment would remain constant at its 1960 level and that industry not reported would maintain its 1960 proportion of total employment. In other words, we applied Almon's growth rate for total civilian employment to industry not reported.

In the case of transportation, our procedure was somewhat different. Almon only has one transportation sector (industry 71 in his model), while we have three (sector 15 through 17). Our procedure in the case of transportation was to constrain the growth rate of the total employment of sectors 15, 16, and 17 to be equal to the growth rate of Almon's industry 71. We thus allowed our model to assign different growth rates to each transportation sector.

Appendix B

Correspondence Between OBE 118-Industry Classification and the 1957 Standard Industrial Classification

OBE 118-Categories Sector	Corresponding 1957 SIC Codes*	OBE 118-Categories Sector	Corresponding 1957 SIC Codes*
1	01, 02, 07, −0713	60	387, 39
2	08	61	n.s.k.(c)
3	09	62	40
4	10	63	421, 423
5	11, 12	64	422
6	13	65	411, 413, 414, 415, 417
7	14	66	412
8	15–17	67	44
9	201	68	45
10	202	69	46
11	203	70	47
12	0713, 204	71	481
13	205	72	482, 489
14	207	73	483
15	208	74	492, 496
16	206, 209, n.s.k.(a)	75	494, 495
17	221–224, 228	76	491, 493, 497
18	225	77	501–509, n.s.k.(d)
19	226	78	54
20	227	79	58
21	229	80	521–524
22	231–238	81	525
23	239	82	533
24	241	83	53, −533
25	242, 243	84	554
26	244, 249	85	55, −554
27	25	86	566
28	27	87	56, −566
29	2823, 2824	88	571
30	285	89	572, 573
31	281, 282, −2823, −2824, 283, 284, 286, 287, 289	90	591
32	3522	91	592
33	357	92	597
34	351, 353–356, 358, 359	93	598
35	36	94	5992
36	371	95	593–596, 599, −5992
37	372	96	n.s.k.(e)
38	373	97	60, 61, 62, 67
39	374, 375, 379	98	63, 64
40	21	99	65, 66
41	261–263, 266	100	70
42	265	101	721, 727
43	264	102	722–726, 729
44	291	103	88
45	295, 299	104	731
46	301–303, 306	105	732–736, 739

Correspondence Between OBE 118-Industry Classification and the 1957 Standard Industrial Classification (continued)

OBE 118-Categories Sector	Corresponding 1957 SIC Codes*	OBE 118-Categories Sector	Corresponding 1957 SIC Codes*
47	307	106	75
48	311	107	76
49	313, 314	108	78, 792
50	312, 315–317, 319	109	791, 793, 794
51	321–323	110	80
52	324, 327	111	82, 84
53	325	112	86
54	326	113	81, 89
55	328, 329	114	9190 part
56	3312, 3313	115	91, −9190 part, 94
57	19, −194, 3315–3317, 332, 3391, 341–349, 333–336, 3392, 3399	116	92, 93
58	n.s.k.(b)	117	9190 part
59	194, 381–386	118	99

The sectoring scheme includes the following categories for which no comparable SIC categories exist:

n.s.k.(a) Not specified food industries
n.s.k.(b) Not specified metal industries
n.s.k.(c) Not specified manufacturing industries
n.s.k.(d) Not specified wholesale trade
n.s.k.(e) Not specified retail trade

* A dash between two SIC numbers is read "through"; a minus preceding a SIC number set off by commas means "delete."

Appendix C

Correspondence Between OBE 32- and OBE 118-Industry Lists

OBE 32-Industry List		OBE 118-Industry List	
No.	Industry	No.	Industry
1	Agriculture	1	Agriculture
2	Forestry and fisheries	2	Forestry
		3	Fisheries
3	Mining	4	Metal mining
		5	Coal mining
		6	Crude petroleum and natural gas extraction
		7	Nonmetallic mining and quarrying, except fuel
4	Contract construction	8	Contract construction
5	Food and kindred products	9	Meat products
		10	Dairy products
		11	Canning and preserving fruits, vegetables and sea foods
		12	Grain-mill products
		13	Bakery products
		14	Confectionery and related products
		15	Beverage industries
		16	Misc. and not-specified food and kindred products
6	Textiles	17	Yarn, thread, and fabric mills
		18	Knitting mills
		19	Dyeing and finishing textiles, except wool and knit goods
		20	Floor coverings, except hard surface
		21	Misc. textile-mill products
7	Apparel	22	Apparel and accessories
		23	Misc. fabricated textile products
8	Lumber, wood and furniture products	24	Logging
		25	Sawmills, planing mills, and mill work
		26	Misc. wood products, except furniture and fixtures
		27	Furniture and fixtures
9	Printing and publishing	28	Printing, publishing, and allied industries
10	Chemicals and allied products	29	Synthetic fibers
		30	Paints, varnishes, and related products
		31	Misc. chemical and allied products (including drugs and medicines)
11	Machinery	32	Farm machinery and equipment
		33	Office, computing, and accounting machinery
		34	Misc. machinery, except electrical
		35	Electrical machinery, equipment, and supplies

Correspondence Between OBE 32- and OBE 118-Industry Lists (continued)

OBE 32-Industry List		OBE 118-Industry List	
No.	Industry	No.	Industry
12	Motor vehicles and equipment	36	Motor vehicles and motor vehicle equipment
13	Other transportation equipment	37	Aircraft and aircraft parts
		38	Ship and boat building and repairing
		39	Railroad and misc. transportation equipment
14	Miscellaneous manufacturing	40	Tobacco manufactures
		41	Pulp, paper, and paperboard mills
		42	Paperboard containers and boxes
		43	Misc. paper and pulp products
		44	Petroleum refining
		45	Misc. petroleum and coal products
		46	Rubber products
		47	Misc. plastic products
		48	Leather: tanned, cured, and finished
		49	Footwear, except rubber
		50	Leather products, except footwear
		51	Glass and glass products
		52	Cement, concrete, gypsum, and plaster products
		53	Structural clay products
		54	Pottery and related products
		55	Misc. nonmetallic mineral and stone products
		56	Blast furnaces, steel works, rolling and finishing mills
		57	Other primary metal and fabricated metal industries
		58	Not-specified metal industries
		59	Professional and photographic equipment and supplies
		60	Watches, clocks, etc., and misc. manufacturing industries
		61	Not-specified manufacturing industries
15	Railroad	62	Railroads and railway express service
16	Trucking and warehousing	63	Trucking service
		64	Warehousing and storage
17	Other transportation	65	Street railways and bus lines
		66	Taxicab service
		67	Water transportation
		68	Air transportation
		69	Petroleum and gasoline pipelines
		70	Services incidental to transportation
18	Communications	71	Telephone (wire and radio)
		72	Telegraph (wire and radio)
		73	Radio broadcasting and TV

Correspondence Between OBE 32- and OBE 118-Industry Lists (continued)

OBE 32-Industry List		OBE 118-Industry List	
No.	Industry	No.	Industry
19	Utilities	74	Gas and steam supply systems
		75	Water supply and sanitary services
		76	Electric, electric-gas, other and not-specified utilities
20	Wholesale trade	77	Wholesale trade
21	Food and dairy products stores	78	Food and dairy products stores
22	Eating and drinking places	79	Eating and drinking places
23	Other retail trade	80	Lumber and building material retailing
		81	Hardware and farm equipment stores
		82	Limited price variety stores
		83	General merchandise retailing
		84	Gasoline service stations
		85	Motor vehicles and accessories retailing
		86	Shoe stores
		87	Apparel and accessories stores, except shoe stores
		88	Furniture and house furnishing stores
		89	Household appliance, TV, and radio stores
		90	Drug stores
		91	Liquor stores
		92	Jewelry stores
		93	Fuel and ice dealers
		94	Retail florists
		95	Misc. retail stores
		96	Not-specified retail trade
24	Finance, insurance, and real estate	97	Banking, credit agencies, and brokerage and investment companies
		98	Insurance
		99	Real estate
25	Hotels and other personal services	100	Hotels and lodging places
		101	Laundering, cleaning, and dyeing services
		102	All other personal services
26	Private households	103	Private households
27	Business and repair services	104	Advertising
		105	Misc. business services
		106	Automobile repair service and garages
		107	Misc. repair service
28	Entertainment and recreation services	108	Theaters and motion pictures
		109	All other entertainment and recreational services

Correspondence Between OBE 32- and OBE 118-Industry Lists (continued)

	OBE 32-Industry List		OBE 118-Industry List
No.	Industry	No.	Industry
29	Medical and other professional services	110	Medical and other health services (including hospitals)
		111	Educational services
		112	Welfare, religious, and nonprofit membership organizations
		113	Legal, engineering, and misc. professional services
30	Public administration	114	Postal service
		115	Federal public administration
		116	State and local public administration
31	Armed Forces	117	Armed Forces
32	Industry not reported	118	Industry not reported

A list of the Standard Industrial Classification industries included in each of the above section is presented in Appendix B.

Appendix D
Estimated Equations

I. Explanatory Variables Appearing in Equations[1]

Variable Number	Brief Description[2]
1	Ln employment in agriculture
2	Ln employment in forestry and fisheries
3	Ln employment in the mining Industry
4	Ln employment in contract construction
5	Ln employment in food and kindred products
6	Ln employment in textile-mill products
7	Ln employment in apparel manufacturing
8	Ln employment in lumber and wood products
9	Ln employment in printing and publishing
10	Ln employment in chemicals and allied products
11	Ln employment in electrical and other machinery
12	Ln employment in motor vehicles and equipment
13	Ln employment in other transportation equipment
14	Ln employment in other and miscellaneous manufacturing
15	Ln employment in railroads and railway express
16	Ln employment in trucking and warehousing
17	Ln employment in other transportation
18	Ln employment in communications
19	Ln employment in utilities
20	Ln employment in population oriented services – A
21	Ln employment in population oriented services – B
22	Ln employment in public administration
111	Special agriculture variable
115	Population 1950/population 1940
116	Proportion population nonwhite
117	Population density
118	Proportion population urban
119	Proportion population rural farm
120	Proportion population aged 21–64 years
121	Ln population aged 21–64 years
122	Live births per family
123	Proportion population >25 years, <5 years education
124	Proportion population >25 years, <12 years education
125	Proportion labor force male
126	Proportion labor force unemployed
127	Proportion of employed in mining
128	Proportion of employed in manufacturing
129	Proportion of employed in wholesale and retail trade
130	Average family size
131	Median family income
133	Proportion dwelling units built since 1940
134	Time and savings deposits per capita
135	Normal maximum temperature
136	Normal precipitation
137	Distance to nearest SMSA >250,000 population

[1] All data for 1950 unless otherwise noted.

[2] A more detailed description of each variable may be found in Table 5–1.

I. Explanatory Variables Appearing in Equations[1] (continued)

Variable Number	Brief Description[2]
138	Distance to nearest SMSA >1,000,000 population
139	Terrain variability index
140	Relative extent of unionization, 1953
142	Highways variable
143	Cost of oil, 1958
144	Cost of gas, 1958
145	Cost of electricity, 1958
147	Median age
148	Land area
149	Ln total employment
150	Average employment per manufacturing establishment
152	Intercept dummy for sector 5
154	Intercept dummy for sector 11
164	Slope dummy for sector 11
165	Slope dummy for sector 13
168	Slope dummy for sector 14

II. Estimated Equations

Industry Number	Name	Type of Equation	Number of Observations	Degrees of Freedom	F-Statistic	$R^2(C)$	Standard Error	Independent Variable	Coefficient	t-Statistic	Beta Weight
1	Agriculture	R_2	3097	3077	$F(19,3077) = 1849.3533$	0.9190	0.2824	Constant	-0.9970	1.21	
								111	0.01654	55.77	
								1	0.9575	2.61	
								118	0.07245	1.05	
								117	0.00000015	9.00	
								131	0.00009724	-7.37	
								139	-0.005542	-14.09	
								127	-1.1983	6.51	
								144	0.1813	1.59	
								124	0.1397	5.55	
								120	0.9550	-2.69	
								116	-0.1115	-15.06	
								128	-0.8710	13.85	
								115	0.4891	-13.81	
								133	-0.9665	7.43	
								138	0.0003954	1.24	
								137	0.0001081	3.09	
								134	0.0001088	-5.30	
								130	-0.08168	-1.71	
								143	-0.02250		
4	Contract construction	R_2	3097	3084	$F(12,3084) = 3796.7704$	0.9363	0.3258	Constant	-1.1306	8.13	
								133	0.6110	-6.84	
								137	-0.0007043	37.19	
								4	0.7038	14.96	
								121	0.2761	-5.53	
								131	-0.00006287	5.50	
								129	1.05782	3.94	
								115	0.1500	4.18	
								128	0.2643	3.93	
								138	0.0002237	3.11	
								136	0.002112	1.40	
								145	0.002655	1.23	
								144	0.03735		

	Industry	Model	N	df	F	R²	R² (2)	Variable	Coef.	t	β
5	Food and kindred products	D_1	78	75	$F_{(2,75)} = 9.2402$	0.1656	0.4216	Constant	−1.2143		
								115	0.9283	2.97	0.3432
								149	0.1074	1.46	0.1685
		D_2	3019	3012	$F_{(6,3012)} = 72.6736$	0.1244	0.1666	Constant	0.8376		
								116	0.05423	2.55	0.0521
								5	0.03800	15.05	0.3888
								131	−0.00001051	−2.00	−0.0493
								133	0.05492	1.94	0.0349
								138	−0.00007296	−3.03	−0.0573
								118	−0.04805	−2.76	−0.0732
		R_1	24	17	$F_{(6,17)} = 5.0754$	0.4942	0.3166	Constant	0.5144		
								148	0.0002096	3.00	
								118	−0.7004	−1.71	
								119	−1.6028	−2.70	
								126	−7.2654	−1.98	
								115	0.6970	1.60	
								143	0.4242	1.96	
		R_2	2920	2907	$F_{(12,2907)} = 1951.4772$	0.8891	0.5596	Constant	−1.6809		
								5	0.7338	57.40	
								149	0.3258	15.90	
								127	−0.9403	−5.47	
								115	0.3024	5.44	
								152	0.6243	4.18	
								131	−0.00008595	−3.79	
								126	−1.8491	−3.27	
								143	0.0809	3.00	
								116	−0.2391	−2.60	
								122	0.9526	1.75	
								139	−0.002311	−1.57	
								119	0.1124	1.12	
6	Textiles	D_1	890	884	$F_{(5,884)} = 14.8297$	0.0711	0.3415	Constant	−0.6802		
								121	0.09311	5.75	0.2079
								127	−0.3749	−2.97	−0.0968
								142	0.02228	2.25	0.0774
								144	0.1252	1.75	0.0575
								137	−0.0002011	−1.68	−0.0580

II. Estimated Equations (continued)

Industry Number	Name	Type of Equation	Number of Observations	Degrees of Freedom	F-Statistic	$R^2(C)$	Standard Error	Independent Variable	Coefficient	t-Statistic	Beta Weight
		D_2	2207	2201	$F(5,2201) = 208.4232$	0.3195	0.3869	Constant	-0.1730		
								6	0.08534	22.51	0.4806
								121	0.08082	6.99	0.1853
								119	0.2361	4.15	0.0997
								147	-0.009085	-3.86	-0.0744
								117	-0.00000725	-2.04	-0.0372
		R_1	131	125	$F(5,125) = 6.8131$	0.1764	0.8453	Constant	-1.2853		
								129	-5.5166	-3.43	
								121	0.4382	3.17	
								140	-0.006755	-2.62	
								142	0.1183	2.01	
								144	0.6912	1.46	
		R_2	1486	1478	$F(7,1478) = 793.5142$	0.7887	1.0352	Constant	1.05782		
								6	0.7200	54.51	
								129	-5.9458	-7.68	
								144	0.6862	5.66	
								149	0.1886	4.94	
								143	-0.2472	-3.79	
								134	-0.0003772	-3.22	
								127	-1.7304	-2.91	
7	Apparel	D_1	820	811	$F(8,811) = 33.7005$	0.2412	0.3882	Constant	-0.8030		
								121	0.1156	5.06	0.2098
								136	0.008518	7.26	0.2857
								118	0.2771	3.40	0.1347
								131	-0.00006106	-3.33	-0.1311
								150	0.001356	2.59	0.0837
								119	0.2050	2.21	0.0834
								122	-0.7867	-1.69	-0.0523
								145	-0.003548	-1.12	-0.0356

Sector	n	df	F			Variable	Coefficient	t	β
D_2	2277	2269	$F(7,2269) = 133.2993$	0.2889	0.2900	Constant	0.6588		
						7	0.06142	20.78	0.4121
						131	−0.0001049	−11.48	−0.2535
						137	−0.001050	−9.31	−0.1795
						115	0.1771	5.85	0.1260
						139	−0.003788	−4.43	−0.0829
						143	0.05115	3.40	0.0624
						145	0.003098	1.23	0.0240
R_1	224	217	$F(6,217) = 20.7728$	0.3443	1.1593	Constant	−2.5222		
						131	−0.0007037	−5.86	
						142	0.1824	2.76	
						150	0.008060	2.36	
						119	1.2309	2.25	
						128	1.3787	1.49	
						149	0.6087	4.64	
R_2	1965	1955	$F(9,1955) = 565.2971$	0.7210	0.9362	Constant	−0.3183		
						7	0.6297	49.08	
						123	4.05947	10.64	
						149	0.3997	12.20	
						129	−5.2476	−8.07	
						128	−1.1964	−5.63	
						134	−0.0002821	−2.63	
						144	0.3479	3.39	
						122	−7.4499	−5.74	
						116	−0.2432	−1.29	
8 Lumber, wood and furniture									
D_1	180	177	$F(2,177) = 8.0049$	0.0674	0.3340	Constant	−0.7154		
						74	2.7550	2.36	0.1703
						126	0.1020	3.13	0.2257
						121			
D_2	2917	2911	$F(5,2911) = 278.8133$	0.3224	0.2317	Constant	0.5937		
						8	0.07014	27.30	0.4931
						137	−0.0006145	−9.52	−0.1594
						144	−0.05685	−2.64	−0.0418
						124	0.09688	2.25	0.0386
						116	−0.04357	−1.51	−0.0268

II. Estimated Equations (continued)

Industry Number	Name	Type of Equation	Number of Observations	Degrees of Freedom	F-Statistic	$R^2(C)$	Standard Error	Independent Variable	Coefficient	t-Statistic	Beta Weight
		R_1	25	16	$F(8,16) = 2.8079$	0.3500	0.3702	Constant	−6.9741		
								119	2.6109	3.47	
								149	0.5240	3.01	
								135	0.03283	2.39	
								115	0.8987	1.89	
								116	−6.7973	−1.76	
								145	0.02962	1.77	
								139	0.01628	1.22	
								127	1.4107	1.38	
		R_2	2664	2655	$F(8,2655) = 2162.0840$	0.8665	0.5886	Constant	0.8863		
								8	0.8599	116.76	
								135	−0.01118	−7.24	
								115	0.2868	5.10	
								142	0.03351	4.73	
								127	−0.7664	−4.28	
								139	0.006335	3.99	
								145	−0.01246	−2.85	
								119	0.2439	3.22	
9	Printing and publishing	D_1	36	28	$F(7,28) = 3.4549$	0.3101	0.3453	Constant	−1.4561		
								144	1.4648	3.37	0.7162
								117	−0.01568	−2.42	−0.5402
								121	0.1128	1.23	0.2791
								143	−0.1784	−1.09	−0.1889
								124	1.2056	2.11	0.3927
								134	−0.005400	−1.60	−0.3712
								129	5.1483	1.79	0.3087

D_2	3061	3050	$F(10,3050) = 42.1690$	0.1183	0.1995	Constant	0.08903		
						121	0.05218	9.73	0.2810
						129	0.7367	5.81	0.1554
						131	0.00004154	5.73	0.1669
						118	-0.1060	-4.40	-0.1355
						143	0.03349	3.87	0.0694
						136	0.001220	3.26	0.0786
						124	0.1430	2.57	0.0743
						134	-0.00005288	-2.30	-0.0542
						122	-0.2909	-1.83	-0.0331
						117	-0.00000328	-1.61	-0.0316

R_1	8	7	$F(0,7) = 0$	0	0.4813	Constant	1.8048	
R_2	2916	2905	$F(10,2905) = 2885.6358$	0.9082	0.5050	Constant	-1.4731	
						115	0.4536	7.16
						124	-0.9197	-6.64
						137	-0.005940	-4.20
						9	0.5950	28.64
						121	0.4156	15.28
						145	0.008824	2.71
						122	-1.2909	-2.84
						119	-0.3997	-5.29
						139	-0.003852	-3.00
						133	-0.3286	-2.61

10	Chemicals and allied products									
	D_1	454	448	$F(5,448) = 17.0473$	0.1486	0.4111	Constant	-1.3739		
							115	0.3008	2.89	0.1497
							145	-0.01246	-2.91	-0.1284
							131	-0.00006411	-3.07	-0.1485
							121	0.2088	7.96	0.3764
							133	-0.2085	-1.01	-0.0513

II. Estimated Equations (continued)

Industry Number	Name	Type of Equation	Number of Observations	Degrees of Freedom	F-Statistic	$R^2(C)$	Standard Error	Independent Variable	Coefficient	t-Statistic	Beta Weight
		D_2	2643	2635	$F(7, 2635) = 105.7738$	0.2170	0.3444	Constant	0.1537	10.70	
								10	0.05445	-8.38	0.2912
								131	-0.0001025	-3.13	-0.2168
								133	-0.2648	5.59	-0.0779
								128	0.3740	4.25	0.1217
								149	0.04449	5.22	0.1227
								115	0.2392	2.13	0.1539
								129	0.4483		0.0518
		R_1	124	120	$F(3, 120) = 6.2400$	0.1061	0.9471	Constant	0.4876		
								115	0.6737	2.64	
								128	1.01844	1.05	
								122	8.7073	2.67	
		R_2	2151	2144	$F(6, 2144) = 869.1511$	0.7077	1.0276	Constant	-0.1211		
								10	0.6669	47.62	
								128	1.3084	6.38	
								137	-0.002459	-6.05	
								115	0.9060	9.47	
								143	0.1892	3.44	
								142	0.02682	2.03	
11	Machinery	D_1	211	207	$F(3, 207) = 16.3164$	0.1756	0.4484	Constant	-0.8119		
								149	0.2293	5.36	0.3518
								137	-0.0008769	-3.20	-0.2052
								115	-0.3002	-1.91	-0.1224
		D_2	2886	2875	$F(10, 2875) = 61.0241$	0.1719	0.2689	Constant	0.5184		
								137	-0.0007685	-9.53	-0.1969
								149	0.04394	5.02	0.1625
								11	0.02290	4.81	0.1760
								123	-0.6342	-4.67	-0.2308
								164	1.7193	3.81	0.1937
								154	-0.2117	-3.01	-0.0944
								133	0.08223	1.65	0.0318
								131	-0.00002045	-1.80	-0.0572
								124	0.1519	1.75	0.0564
								139	-0.0008519	-1.28	-0.0229

107

						Variable	Coefficient	t	
R_1	89	85	$F(3,85) = 5.1220$	0.1132	0.8103	Constant 33	−1.9676		
						149	0.5881	3.73	
						131	−0.0001587	−1.62	
						116	−0.7776	−1.55	
R_2	2607	2597	$F(9,2597) = 1536.4499$	0.8413	0.8582	Constant 33	−2.6504		
						11	0.6723	44.86	
						121	0.3510	11.83	
						115	0.4522	5.58	
						137	−0.002772	−8.94	
						143	0.3159	7.46	
						136	0.008972	5.09	
						119	0.2240	1.66	
						123	−1.3732	−6.38	
						127	−0.7687	−3.05	
12' Motor vehicles and equipment									
D_1	1092	1085	$F(6,1085) = 27.8724$	0.1280	0.3808	Constant	−0.6541		
						121	0.1208	7.03	0.2394
						131	−0.00006230	−4.21	−0.1407
						137	−0.0003856	−2.57	−0.0932
						140	0.0009824	2.57	0.0779
						138	−0.0002224	−2.39	−0.0865
						118	0.09710	1.58	0.0515
D_2	2005	1997	$F(7,1997) = 106.9732$	0.2698	0.3848	Constant	−0.2569		
						12	0.06037	10.45	0.2962
						137	−0.001186	−7.36	−0.1594
						149	0.08736	6.97	0.2102
						131	−0.0001009	−6.36	−0.1796
						143	0.09425	4.55	0.0902
						116	−0.2665	−3.47	−0.0842
						140	0.001148	3.44	0.0791
R_1	230	226	$F(3,226) = 2.3126$	0.0126	0.6908	Constant 34	1.1768		
						119	0.8375	2.32	
						129	1.9359	1.18	
						148	0.00004363	1.70	

II. Estimated Equations (continued)

Industry Number	Name	Type of Equation	Number of Observations	Degrees of Freedom	F-Statistic	$R^2(C)$	Standard Error	Independent Variable	Coefficient	t-Statistic	Beta Weight
		R_2	1438	1429	$F(8,1429) = 594.5689$	0.7675	0.9529	Constant	−0.8315	−1.88	
								34			
								118	−0.3473	−3.54	
								126	−4.6512	−2.46	
								129	−2.2225	−3.02	
								137	−0.001779	43.58	
								12	0.6890	6.13	
								121	0.2596	2.87	
								140	0.002936	1.39	
								147	0.01202		
13	Other transportation equipment	D_1	1220	1214	$F(5,1214) = 50.8437$	0.1691	0.4343	Constant	−1.09745		
								136	0.008863	8.53	0.2806
								149	0.1332	7.32	0.2249
								119	−0.1469	−1.80	−0.0541
								147	0.004270	1.33	0.0367
								139	0.001626	1.07	0.0295
		D_2	1877	1870	$F(6,1870) = 66.4080$	0.1726	0.3715	Constant	0.4369		
								13	0.05930	11.65	0.3097
								139	−0.004890	−4.36	−0.0935
								128	0.3630	4.26	0.1130
								129	0.9932	3.10	0.1052
								115	0.08142	2.26	0.0539
								118	−0.08193	−1.51	−0.0551
		R_1	425	416	$F(8,416) = 6.5328$	0.0924	1.0340	Constant	−2.9664		
								129	8.7246	4.07	
								119	1.4830	3.05	
								128	1.5353	2.55	
								135	0.02080	2.29	
								133	0.9881	1.62	
								137	−0.001149	−1.32	
								165	−1.02816	−1.01	
								149	0.2021	2.24	

	n	n	F-statistic			Variable	Coefficient	t	
R_2	1480	1472	$F_{(7,1472)} = 441.3396$	0.6755	1.1217	Constant	−2.2276	32.45	
						13	0.6212	7.17	
						121	0.2867	5.60	
						119	1.5687	−5.53	
						137	−0.003432	5.21	
						115	0.6796	3.20	
						129	3.1571	2.68	
						145	0.02958		
14 Miscellaneous manufacturing									
D_1	78	69	$F_{(8,69)} = 6.4349$	0.3526	0.3889	Constant	−4.5704	3.07	0.4324
						168	2.7324	4.00	2.7424
						121	1.7538	−3.27	−2.2336
						149	−1.4340	1.69	0.2338
						120	2.8295	−1.82	−0.1872
						145	−0.01955	1.81	0.2050
						130	0.1572	2.27	0.2315
						138	0.0007598	−1.12	−0.1137
						137	−0.0004706		
D_2	3019	3010	$F_{(8,3010)} = 96.3654$	0.2015	0.1942	Constant	1.1506	−4.41	−0.0768
						125	−0.1399	−4.68	−0.0791
						145	−0.005360	−8.71	−0.1850
						137	−0.0005179	6.46	0.1262
						136	0.002035	6.34	0.1975
						14	0.01836	−4.73	−0.1024
						120	−0.5365	2.09	0.0446
						147	0.002460	1.07	0.0325
						149	0.006344		
R_1	29	24	$F_{(4,24)} = 2.0966$	0.1046	0.5696	Constant	−5.5563	2.43	
						135	0.05589	2.68	
						121	0.5820	1.69	
						138	0.001428	−1.14	
						115	−1.1054		

II. Estimated Equations (continued)

Industry Number	Name	Type of Equation	Number of Observations	Degrees of Freedom	F-Statistic	$R^2(C)$	Standard Error	Independent Variable	Coefficient	t-Statistic	Beta Weight
		R_2	2869	2857	$F(11,2857) = 1933.0806$	0.8811	0.7174	Constant	-2.1205		
								14	0.7568	67.17	
								121	0.2719	11.25	
								127	-1.04541	-5.33	
								115	0.4273	6.95	
								159	0.4093	3.87	
								118	-0.1870	-2.29	
								135	0.01756	7.28	
								168	-1.6661	-3.71	
								138	-0.0001882	-1.60	
								120	-0.5605	-1.23	
								123	0.2800	1.14	
15	Railroads	D_1	60	55	$F(4,55) = 5.7674$	0.2315	0.1911	Constant	0.08290	4.68	
								115	0.3129		0.6191
								149	-0.06652	-2.27	-0.2731
								119	0.1637	1.39	0.1750
								144	0.2114	1.39	0.1631
		D_2	3037	3029	$F(7,3029) = 121.7906$	0.2176	0.1993	Constant	0.9810	22.17	
								15	0.08368	6.33	0.6269
								119	0.1683	-4.77	0.1464
								125	-0.1606	-6.94	-0.0841
								139	-0.003240	2.81	-0.1163
								144	0.05185	3.01	0.0471
								115	0.05481	-7.68	0.0598
								149	-0.04230		-0.2117
		R_1	3	1	$F(1,1) = 59.5539$	0.9505	0.0234	Constant	2.04677		
								149	-0.09035	-7.72	

111

R_2	2874	2864	$F(9,2864) = 3466.7764$	0.9156	0.4672

Variable	Coefficient	t
Constant	-0.7117	102.89
15	0.9290	7.34
112	0.07873	4.38
115	0.1929	-2.33
118	-0.1178	-3.39
128	-0.3408	2.02
131	0.00003800	-2.69
123	-0.3047	-1.53
126	-0.6350	1.13
137	0.0001576	

16   Trucking and warehousing

D_2^*	3090	3079	$F(10,3079) = 38.9512$	0.1091	0.1375

Variable	Coefficient	t	
Constant	0.6940	6.37	
113	0.01509	5.15	0.1968
124	0.2104	-7.76	0.1603
128	-0.2353	11.25	-0.2044
131	0.00005869	-5.47	0.3475
137	-0.0002207	-3.93	-0.1236
127	-0.1576	2.40	-0.0758
119	0.05304	4.71	0.0720
136	0.001364	-1.58	0.1281
140	-0.0001404	-1.81	-0.0309
120	-0.1426		-0.0405

* No D_1 equation.

R_2^*	3023	3009	$F(13,3009) = 1794.5205$	0.8852	0.4761

Variable	Coefficient	t
Constant	-2.04941	9.95
113	0.1285	4.85
115	0.2867	-4.54
118	-0.2757	2.19
128	0.2485	7.27
129	2.4776	33.74
16	0.6207	10.74
149	0.2674	3.11
135	0.004801	3.98
138	0.0003133	-6.86
126	-3.05660	-1.60
124	-0.2072	2.45
127	0.3236	1.27
133	0.1625	

* No R_1 equation.

II. Estimated Equations (continued)

Industry Number	Name	Type of Equation	Number of Observations	Degrees of Freedom	F-Statistic	$R^2(C)$	Standard Error	Independent Variable	Coefficient	t-Statistic	Beta Weight
17	Other transportation	D_1	52	47	$F(4,47) = 3.4021$	0.1420	0.4506	Constant	-1.1153		
								137	-0.001480	-2.28	-0.3222
								149	1.09235	1.77	1.8648
								121	-0.7630	-1.26	-1.3029
								131	-0.00007465	-1.20	-0.2096
		D_2	3045	3037	$F(7,3037) = 70.3304$	0.1372	0.1800	Constant	1.3035		
								114	0.008216	2.66	0.0906
								137	-0.0002659	-5.28	-0.1084
								125	-0.1336	-4.21	-0.0820
								149	-0.1424	-4.71	-0.8288
								17	0.02985	5.95	0.2467
								120	-0.7158	-8.04	-0.1534
								121	0.1362	4.37	0.7963
		R_1	20	15	$F(4,15) = 2.4211$	0.1898	0.5189	Constant	-0.5173		
								143	0.8409	2.49	
								114	0.1570	1.10	
								137	-0.003488	-1.93	
								128	22.5517	2.66	
		R_2	2926	2917	$F(8,2917) = 2291.0818$	0.8623	0.5391	Constant	-1.5171		
								114	0.07061	6.86	
								128	-0.6578	-6.11	
								17	0.6226	37.97	
								121	0.2858	12.29	
								133	0.9825	10.14	
								123	0.5588	5.81	
								127	-0.6870	-4.67	
								143	-0.03886	-1.62	

113

								Variable	Coefficient	t	β
18	Communications	D_1	53	49	$F(3,49) = 4.4332$	0.1493	0.3968	Constant	0.008269		
								119	0.2754	1.17	0.1537
								131	0.0001667	3.24	0.4244
								137	−0.0006400	−1.33	−0.1691
		D_2	3044	3034	$F(9,3034) = 65.7463$	0.1604	0.2127	Constant	0.7214		
								18	0.05877	13.21	0.3996
								131	0.00004565	5.64	0.1670
								119	0.1625	4.80	0.1371
								120	−0.4838	−3.99	−0.0855
								129	0.4347	3.08	0.0838
								136	0.0009790	2.38	0.0574
								134	−0.00008833	−4.05	−0.0829
								116	0.04184	1.50	0.0304
								137	−0.00007264	−1.19	−0.0253
		R_1	13	8	$F(4,8) = 30.4857$	0.9000	0.1552	Constant	−3.8152		
								149	0.7563	6.30	
								115	0.6127	1.27	
								117	−0.007145	−1.96	
								119	−1.07715	−3.42	
		R_2	2870	2857	$F(12,2857) = 1936.0403$	0.8900	0.5094	Constant	−2.1284		
								115	0.4566	7.23	
								117	−0.00001515	−2.89	
								118	0.1713	2.61	
								131	−0.00003105	−1.62	
								18	0.6019	31.39	
								149	0.3846	16.95	
								145	0.003681	1.17	
								119	−0.4280	−4.51	
								148	0.00001098	1.37	
								133	0.1897	1.46	
								134	0.0002026	3.25	
								137	−0.0003722	−2.48	

II. Estimated Equations (continued)

Industry Number	Name	Type of Equation	Number of Observations	Degrees of Freedom	F-Statistic	$R^2(C)$	Standard Error	Independent Variable	Coefficient	t-Statistic	Beta Weight
19	Utilities	D_1	29	23	$F(5,23) = 3.9755$	0.3237	0.3909	Constant	-0.8688		
								85			
								148	-0.0004886	-2.61	-0.4528
								128	1.3334	1.67	0.2864
								115	1.2074	1.38	0.2431
								122	2.9262	1.68	0.2665
								139	0.01018	1.01	0.1658
		D_2	3068	3056	$F(11,3056) = 35.2608$	0.1091	0.1218	Constant	1.2203		
								85			
								19	0.03664	9.15	0.4206
								125	-0.1022	-4.92	-0.0932
								120	-0.2959	-4.04	-0.0949
								119	0.07890	4.28	0.1200
								130	-0.03207	-4.96	-0.1001
								124	0.09849	3.44	0.0844
								139	-0.0006918	-2.42	-0.0439
								148	0.00000489	2.56	0.0498
								121	-0.01512	-3.09	-0.1340
								137	-0.00008750	-2.67	-0.0551
								115	0.02365	2.17	0.0461
		R_1	10	7	$F(2,7) = 5.1665$	0.4231	0.3674	Constant	2.1256		
								126	63.8546	3.08	
								145	-0.07917	-1.14	
		R_2	3016	3008	$F(7,3008) = 3772.5690$	0.8975	0.4555	Constant	-1.7397		
								19	0.7033	46.76	
								149	0.2767	15.63	
								133	0.7359	8.60	
								129	1.2492	5.09	
								135	0.006079	4.88	
								137	-0.0002967	-2.40	
								145	0.003288	1.19	

20	Consumer services	R^2	3097	3082	$F_{(14,3082)} = 5864.8412$	0.9636	0.2597

Constant	-0.1959	
124	-0.8414	-13.37
126	0.9412	4.05
133	1.1114	25.12
137	-0.0004958	-6.97
21	0.2353	11.55
127	-0.3600	-5.04
149	0.7751	35.77
125	-0.2108	-4.80
148	0.00000675	1.61
143	-0.05215	-4.42
139	-0.005959	-9.09
118	0.2921	10.10
116	0.2514	7.54
117	-0.00000647	-2.72

21	Business and professional services	R^2	3097	3085	$F_{(11,3085)} = 12674.2880$	0.9783	0.2033

Constant	-0.2360	
115	0.4767	26.55
124	-0.5898	-8.81
137	-0.0003600	-6.28
21	0.8723	52.76
145	0.006100	5.13
121	0.1171	6.55
128	0.1274	3.35
126	-0.6021	-3.38
136	0.0009405	2.29
123	0.4555	8.31
129	0.5365	4.46

II. Estimated Equations (continued)

Industry Number	Name	Type of Equation	Number of Observations	Degrees of Freedom	F-Statistic	$R^2(C)$	Standard Error	Independent Variable	Coefficient	t-Statistic	Beta Weight
22	Public administration	R_2	3097	3082	$F(14,3082) = 4145.4197$	0.9493	0.2992	Constant	-1.2587		
								22	0.8855	62.54	
								115	0.3135	11.53	
								121	0.1033	6.96	
								135	0.006209	6.05	
								124	-0.4519	-4.74	
								120	0.7987	4.51	
								145	0.006479	3.69	
								126	0.9566	3.58	
								127	-0.2729	-3.44	
								123	0.3357	3.14	
								130	0.05095	3.02	
								118	-0.1020	-3.01	
								117	-0.00000757	-2.44	
								134	0.00004461	1.21	

Appendix E
Forecasting Equations

Industry*	D_1 Independent Variable	Coefficient	D_2 Independent Variable	Coefficient	R_1 Independent Variable	Coefficient	R_2 Independent Variable	Coefficient
1	No equation		No equation		No equation		Constant	-0.9970
							111	0.01654
							1	0.9575
							118	0.06633
							117	0.00000013
							131	0.00005279
							139	-0.005542
							127	-1.198
							144	0.05992
							124	0.1558
							120	1.024
							116	-0.1715
							128	-0.7932
							115	0.4726
							133	-0.7275
							138	0.0003954
							137	0.0001081
							134	0.00005523
							130	-0.08085
							143	-0.02039
4	No equation		No equation		No equation		Constant	-1.131
							133	0.4599
							137	-0.0007043
							4	0.7038
							121	0.2761
							131	-0.00003413
							129	1.035
							115	0.1449
							128	0.2407
							138	0.0002237
							136	0.002112
							145	0.002786
							144	0.01235

Forecasting Equations (continued)

Industry*	D₁ Independent Variable	D₁ Coefficient	D₂ Independent Variable	D₂ Coefficient	R₁ Independent Variable	R₁ Coefficient	R₂ Independent Variable	R₂ Coefficient
5	Constant	-1.214	Constant	0.8376	Constant	0.5144	Constant	-1.681
	115	0.8970	116	0.05423	148	-0.0002096	5	0.7338
	149	0.1074	5	0.0380	118	-0.6413	149	0.3258
			131	-0.00000571	119	-3.270	127	0.9403
			133	0.04134	126	-6.838	115	0.2922
			138	-0.00007296	115	6.735	152	0.6243
			118	-0.04399	143	0.3843	131	-0.00004666
							126	-1.740
							143	0.07324
							116	-0.2391
							122	0.9366
							139	-0.002312
							119	0.2293
6	Constant	-0.6802	Constant	-0.1730	Constant	-1.285	Constant	1.058
	121	0.09311	6	0.08534	129	-5.398	6	0.7200
	127	-0.3749	121	0.08082	121	0.4382	129	-5.819
	142	0.02228	119	0.4817	140	-0.006755	144	0.2268
	144	0.04140	147	-0.009301	142	0.1183	149	0.1886
	137	-0.0002011	117	-0.00000610	144	0.2285	143	0.2239
							134	0.0001915
							127	-1.730
7	Constant	-0.8030	Constant	0.6588	Constant	-2.522	Constant	-0.3183
	121	0.1156	7	0.06142	131	-0.0003820	7	0.6297
	136	0.008518	131	-0.00005695	142	0.1824	123	5.364
	118	0.2537	137	0.001050	150	0.009268	149	0.3997
	131	-0.00003315	115	0.1711	119	2.511	129	-5.135
	150	0.001559	139	-0.003788	128	1.256	128	-1.090
	119	0.4182	143	0.04633	149	0.6087	134	-0.0001432
	122	-0.7735	145	0.003251			144	0.1150
	145	-0.003723					122	-7.325
							116	-0.2432

	Constant		Constant		Constant	
8		−0.7154	Constant	0.5937	Constant	−6.974
	126	2.593	8	0.07014	119	5.326
	121	0.1020	137	−0.0006145	149	0.5240
			144	−0.01879	135	0.03283
			124	0.1081	115	0.8683
			116	−0.04357	116	−6.797
					145	0.03109
					139	0.01628
					127	1.411

			Constant			Constant	
		0.8863	8	0.8599			

Constant — 8:
0.8863, 8:0.8599, 135:−0.01118, 115:−0.2771, 142:0.03351, 127:−0.7664, 139:0.006335, 145:−0.01308, 119:0.4975

9:
Constant −1.456
144 0.4842
117 −0.01320
121 0.1128
143 −0.1616
124 1.345
134 −0.002742
129 5.038

Constant 0.08903
121 0.05218
129 0.7210
131 0.00002255
118 −0.09701
143 0.03034
136 0.001220
124 0.1595
134 −0.00002685
122 −0.2860
117 −0.00000276

Constant 1.792

Constant −1.473
115 0.4383
137 −0.0005940
9 −0.5950
121 0.4156
145 0.009261
122 −1.269
119 −0.8155
139 −0.003852
133 −0.2474
124 1.026

10:
Constant −1.374
115 0.2907
145 −0.01308
131 −0.00003481
121 0.2088
133 −0.1570

Constant 0.1537
10 0.05445
131 −0.00005562
133 −0.1994
128 0.3406
149 0.0445
115 0.2311
129 0.4387

Constant 0.4876
115 0.6509
128 0.9275
122 8.561

Constant −0.1211
10 0.6669
128 1.192
137 −0.002459
115 0.8754
143 0.1714
142 0.02682

11:
Constant −0.8119
149 0.2293
137 −0.0008769
115 −0.2901

Constant 0.5184
137 −0.0007685
149 0.04394
11 0.02290
123 −0.8380
164 2.272
154 −0.2117
133 0.06190
131 −0.00001110
124 0.1694
139 −0.0008519

Constant −1.968
149 0.5881
131 −0.0008618
116 −0.7776

Constant −2.650
11 0.6723
121 0.3510
115 0.4369
137 −0.002772
143 0.2862
136 0.008972
119 0.4570
123 −1.815
127 −0.7687

Forecasting Equations (continued)

Industry*	D_1 Independent Variable	Coefficient	D_2 Independent Variable	Coefficient	R_1 Independent Variable	Coefficient	R_2 Independent Variable	Coefficient
12	Constant	-0.6541	Constant	-0.2569	Constant	1.177	Constant	-0.8315
	121	0.1208	12	0.06037	119	1.709	118	-0.3180
	131	-0.00003382	137	-0.001186	129	1.895	126	-4.378
	137	-0.0003856	149	0.08736	148	0.00004363	129	-2.175
	140	-0.0009824	131	-0.00005476			137	-0.001779
	138	-0.0002224	143	0.08538			12	0.6890
	118	0.08891	116	-0.2665			121	0.2596
			140	0.001148			140	0.002936
							147	0.01230
13	Constant	-1.097	Constant	0.4369	Constant	-2.966	Constant	-2.228
	136	0.008863	13	0.05930	129	8.538	13	0.6212
	149	0.1332	139	-0.004890	119	3.025	121	0.2867
	119	-0.2997	128	0.3306	128	1.398	119	3.200
	147	0.004371	129	0.9720	135	0.02080	137	-0.003432
	139	0.001626	115	0.07867	133	0.7438	115	0.6567
			118	-0.07502	137	-0.001149	129	3.090
					165	-1.359	145	0.03104
					149	0.2021		
14	Constant	-4.570	Constant	1.151	Constant	-5.556	Constant	-2.121
	168	3.611	125	-0.1639	135	0.05589	14	0.7568
	121	1.754	145	-0.005625	121	0.5820	121	0.2719
	149	-1.434	137	-0.0005179	138	0.001428	127	-1.045
	120	3.034	136	0.002035	115	-1.068	115	0.4129
	145	-0.02052	14	0.01836			159	0.4093
	130	0.1556	120	-0.5753			118	-0.1712
	138	0.0007598	147	0.002519			135	0.01756
	137	0.0004706	149	0.006344			168	-2.202
							138	-0.0001882
							120	-0.6010
							123	0.3699

15

Constant	0.0829
115	0.3024
149	-0.06652
119	0.3340
144	0.06990

Constant	0.9810
15	0.08368
119	0.3433
125	-0.1880
139	-0.003240
144	0.01714
115	0.05296
149	-0.04230

Constant	2.047
149	-0.09035

Constant	-0.7117
15	0.9290
112	0.0787
115	-0.1864
118	-0.1079
128	-0.3104
131	0.00002063
123	-0.4026
126	-0.5976
137	0.0001576

16

No equation

Constant	0.6940
113	0.01509
124	0.2347
128	-0.2143
131	0.00003186
137	-0.0002207
127	-0.1576
119	0.1082
136	0.001364
140	-0.0001404
120	-0.1529

No equation

Constant	-2.049
113	0.1285
115	0.2770
118	-0.2524
128	0.2263
129	2.425
16	0.6207
149	0.2674
135	0.004801
138	0.0003133
126	-2.877
124	-0.2311
127	0.3236
133	0.1223

17

Constant	-1.115
137	-0.001480
149	1.092
121	-0.7630
131	-0.00004503

Constant	1.304
114	0.008216
137	-0.0002659
125	-0.1565
149	-0.1424
17	0.02985
120	-0.7675
121	0.1362

Constant	-0.5173
143	0.7618
114	0.1570
137	-0.003488
128	20.54

Constant	-1.517
114	0.07061
128	-0.5990
17	0.6226
121	0.2858
133	0.7396
123	0.7384
127	-0.6870
143	-0.03520

Forecasting Equations (continued)

Industry*	D_1 Independent Variable	Coefficient	D_2 Independent Variable	Coefficient	R_1 Independent Variable	Coefficient	R_2 Independent Variable	Coefficient
18	Constant	0.008269	Constant	0.7214	Constant	-3.815	Constant	-2.128
	119	0.5618	18	0.05877	149	0.7563	115	0.4412
	131	0.00009050	131	0.00002478	115	0.5920	117	-0.00001276
	137	-0.0006400	119	0.3313	117	-0.006016	118	0.1568
			120	-0.5187	119	-2.197	131	-0.00001686
			129	0.4254			18	0.6019
			136	0.0009790			149	0.3846
			134	0.00004485			145	0.003863
			116	0.04184			119	-0.8730
			137	-0.00007264			148	0.00001098
							133	0.1428
							134	0.0001029
							137	-0.0003722
19	Constant	-0.8688	Constant	1.220	Constant	2.126	Constant	-1.740
	148	-0.0004886	19	0.03664	126	60.10	19	0.7033
	128	1.214	125	-0.1197	143	-0.08309	149	0.2767
	115	1.167	120	-0.3173			133	0.5539
	122	2.877	119	0.1610			129	1.222
	139	0.01018	130	-0.03175			135	0.006079
			124	0.1099			137	-0.0002967
			139	-0.0006918			145	0.003451
			148	0.00000489				
			121	-0.01512				
			137	-0.00008750				
			115	0.02285				
20	No equation		No equation		No equation		Constant	-0.1959
							124	-0.9385
							126	0.8859
							133	0.8366
							137	-0.0004958
							21	0.2353
							127	-0.3599
							149	0.7751
							125	-0.2469
							148	0.00000675
							143	-0.04724
							139	-0.005959
							118	0.2674
							116	0.2514
							117	-0.00000545

15

Constant	0.0829	Constant	0.9810
115	0.3024	15	0.08368
149	−0.06652	119	0.3433
119	0.3340	125	−0.1880
144	0.06990	139	−0.003240
		144	0.01714
		115	0.05296
		149	−0.04230

Constant	2.047	Constant	−0.7117
149	−0.09035	15	0.9290
		112	0.0787
		115	−0.1864
		118	−0.1079
		128	−0.3104
		131	0.00002063
		123	−0.4026
		126	−0.5976
		137	0.0001576

16

No equation

Constant	0.6940	Constant	−2.049
113	0.01509	113	0.1285
124	0.2347	115	0.2770
128	−0.2143	118	−0.2524
131	0.00003186	128	0.2263
137	−0.0002207	129	2.425
127	−0.1576	16	0.6207
119	0.1082	149	0.2674
136	0.001364	135	0.004801
140	−0.0001404	138	0.0003133
120	−0.1529	126	−2.877
		124	−0.2311
		127	0.3236
		133	0.1223

No equation

17

Constant	−1.115	Constant	1.304
137	−0.001480	114	0.008216
149	1.092	137	−0.0002659
121	−0.7630	125	−0.1565
131	−0.00004503	149	−0.1424
		17	0.02985
		120	−0.7675
		121	0.1362

Constant	−0.5173	Constant	−1.517
143	0.7618	114	0.07061
114	0.1570	128	−0.5990
137	−0.003488	17	0.6226
128	20.54	121	0.2858
		133	0.7396
		123	0.7384
		127	−0.6870
		143	−0.03520

Forecasting Equations (continued)

Industry*	D_1 Independent Variable	Coefficient	D_2 Independent Variable	Coefficient	R_1 Independent Variable	Coefficient	R_2 Independent Variable	Coefficient
18	Constant	0.008269	Constant	0.7214	Constant	−3.815	Constant	−2.128
	119	0.5618	18	0.05877	149	0.7563	115	0.4412
	131	0.00009050	131	0.00002478	115	0.5920	117	−0.00001276
	137	−0.0006400	119	0.3313	117	−0.006016	118	0.1568
			120	−0.5187	119	−2.197	131	−0.00001686
			129	0.4254			18	0.6019
			136	0.0009790			149	0.3846
			134	0.00004485			145	0.003863
			116	0.04184			119	−0.8730
			137	−0.00007264			148	0.00001098
							133	0.1428
							134	0.0001029
							137	−0.0003722
19	Constant	−0.8688	Constant	1.220	Constant	2.126	Constant	−1.740
	148	−0.0004886	19	0.03664	126	60.10	19	0.7033
	128	1.214	125	−0.1197	143	−0.08309	149	0.2767
	115	1.167	120	−0.3173			133	0.5539
	122	2.877	119	0.1610			129	1.222
	139	0.01018	130	−0.03175			135	0.006079
			124	0.1099			137	−0.0002967
			139	−0.0006918			145	0.003451
			148	0.00000489				
			121	−0.01512				
			137	−0.00008750				
			115	0.02285				
20	No equation		No equation		No equation		Constant	−0.1959
							124	−0.9385
							126	0.8859
							133	0.8366
							137	−0.0004958
							21	0.2353
							127	−0.3599
							149	0.7751
							125	−0.2469
							148	0.00000675
							143	−0.04724
							139	−0.005959
							118	0.2674
							116	0.2514
							117	−0.00000545

21	No equation	No equation	No equation		

Variable	Coefficient
Constant	-0.2360
115	0.4606
124	-0.6579
137	-0.0003600
21	0.8723
145	0.006402
121	0.1171
128	0.1160
126	-0.5667
136	0.0009405
123	0.6019
129	-0.5251

22	No equation	No equation	No equation		

Variable	Coefficient
Constant	-1.259
22	0.8855
115	0.3029
121	0.1033
135	0.006209
124	-0.5041
120	0.8564
145	0.006800
126	0.9003
127	-0.2729
123	0.4436
130	0.05044
118	-0.09337
117	-0.00000637
134	0.00002265

* Special analysis was conducted for industries 2, 3, 23 and 24.

D_1: Discriminant equation, (0, 1) case.
D_2: Discriminant equation, (1, 0) case.
R_1: Regression equation for counties with no 1950 employment which pass the D_1 test.
R_2: Regression equation for counties with positive employment in 1950 which pass the D_2 test.